The Idea of Progress
Since the Renaissance

MAJOR ISSUES IN HISTORY

Editor
C. WARREN HOLLISTER,
University of California, Santa Barbara

The Idea of Progress
Since the Renaissance

EDITED BY

W. Warren Wagar

John Wiley & Sons, Inc.
New York London Sydney Toronto

Library of Congress Catalog Card Number: 76-81337
SBN 471 91350 2 (cloth)
SBN 471 91351 0 (paper)
10 9 8 7 6 5 4 3 2 1

Printed in the United States of America

To Winnie

SERIES PREFACE

The reading program in a history survey course traditionally has consisted of a large two-volume textbook and, perhaps, a book of readings. This simple reading program requires few decisions and little imagination on the instructor's part, and tends to encourage in the student the virtue of careful memorization. Such programs are by no means things of the past, but they certainly do not represent the wave of the future.

The reading program in survey courses at many colleges and universities today is far more complex. At the risk of over-simplification, and allowing for many exceptions and overlaps, it can be divided into four categories: (1) textbook, (2) original source readings, (3) specialized historical essays and interpretive studies, and (4) historical problems.

After obtaining an overview of the course subject matter (textbook), sampling the original sources, and being exposed to selective examples of excellent modern historical writing (historical essays), the student can turn to the crucial task of weighing various possible interpretations of major historical issues. It is at this point that memory gives way to creative critical thought. The "problems approach," in other words, is the intellectual climax of a thoughtfully conceived reading program and is, indeed, the most characteristic of all approaches to historical pedagogy among the newer generation of college and university teachers.

The historical problems books currently available are many and varied. Why add to this information explosion? Because the Wiley Major Issues Series constitutes an endeavor to produce something new that will respond to pedagogical needs thus far unmet. First, it is a series of individual volumes—one per problem. Many good teachers would much prefer to select their own historical issues rather than be tied to an inflexible sequence of issues imposed by a publisher and bound together between two covers. Second, the Wiley Major Issues Series is based on the idea of approaching the significant problems of history through a deft interweaving of primary sources and secondary analysis, fused together by the skill of a scholar-editor. It is felt that the essence of a historical issue cannot be satisfactorily probed either by placing a body of undigested source materials into the hands of inexperienced students or by limiting these students to the controversial literature of modern scholars who debate the meaning of sources the student never sees. This series approaches historical problems by exposing students to both the finest historical thinking on the issue and some of the evidence on which this thinking is based. This synthetic approach should prove far more fruitful than either the raw-source approach or the exclusively second-hand approach, for it combines the advantages—and avoids the serious disadvantages—of both.

Finally, the editors of the individual volumes in the Major Issues Series have been chosen from among the ablest scholars in their fields. Rather than faceless referees, they are historians who know their issues from the inside and, in most instances, have themselves contributed significantly to the relevant scholarly literature. It has been the editorial policy of this series to permit the editor-scholars of the individual volumes the widest possible latitude both in formulating their topics and in organizing their materials. Their scholarly competence has been unquestioningly respected; they have been encouraged to approach the problems as they see fit. The titles and themes of the series volumes have been suggested in nearly every case by the scholar-editors themselves. The criteria have been (1) that the issue be of relevance to undergraduate lecture courses in history, and (2) that it be an issue which the scholar-editor knows thoroughly and in which he has done creative work. And, in general, the second criterion has been given precedence over the first. In short, the question "What are the significant historical issues today?" has been answered not by general editors or sales departments but by the scholar-teachers who are responsible for these volumes.

University of California,   *C. Warren Hollister*
Santa Barbara

CONTENTS

The Idea of Progress
Since the Renaissance

INTRODUCTION

The scholar in search of continuing themes in the history of Western civilization is confronted with two quite different types of material: patterns of action, on the one hand, and patterns of thought, on the other.[1] The socioeconomic condition of the peasantry, political revolution, and church-state conflict illustrate problems in the history of action. But historians are coming more and more to acknowledge the importance of continuing themes in the history of Western thought, both for their influence on patterns of action and for their own intrinsic value. A thought is fully as much an event as a war, and thinking falls into observable patterns which, in turn, have histories of their own, no less a part of the ongoing life of humanity than the more conventional subject matter of historical research.

Few scholars today, for example, would question that the traditional values and beliefs of peasants have some measurable effect on their political, social, and economic behavior. A study of the mind of the peasant in, let us say, eighteenth-century Russia could be just as valuable as a study of Russian agriculture or peasant uprisings in that century. No full understanding of either one is possible without a grasp of the intellectual background. Nor is there any reason why the historian should not investigate the leading trends in the history of science, philosophy, theology, and social and political thought, whether they have some immediate relationship to specific so-called historical events or not.

The belief in progress is a good example of a theme in West-

[1] See Benedetto Croce's *La storia come pensiero e come azione*, 1938 ("History as Thought and as Action"), available in English with the title *History as the Story of Liberty*, New York, Norton, 1941. I cannot entirely agree with Croce, but his thesis is at least as defensible as the notion of the orthodox political historian that history consists of political "facts."

I

ern intellectual history that interests the scholar quite apart from its relevance to the history of action. It grows out of concrete circumstances in the life of Western Europe in early modern times, and down through the last two hundred years it has ramified in all directions. Conceptions of progress may be studied in the careers of such varied historical figures as Turgot, Burke, Marx, Darwin, and Lenin. No student of the modern history of religion or industry, socialism or education, metaphysics or nationalism (to cite just a few examples) could avoid making contact with ideas of progress. There is even a formidable literature devoted to the repudiation of the belief in progress, which has its own history and its own heroes.

Ideas of progress have special interest to the historian of the age that stretches from the American and French Revolutions to the outbreak of the first World War. During these years, belief in progress was not so much a sociological or historiographical hypothesis as a credo. It "dominated the European mind to such an extent," writes Christopher Dawson, "that any attempt to question it was regarded as a paradox or a heresy. . . . This creed has played somewhat the same part in our civilization as that taken by religion at other periods of history."[2] By the same token, the history of the West since 1914 is in some measure the history of the disintegration of the progressivist faith, although it dies hard, especially in those parts of the world that imported the belief in progress from Europe, such as the United States and the China of Chairman Mao.

Most scholars agree that ideas of progress did not occur to thinkers in antiquity. If we can define an idea of progress as the judgment that, on balance, history is a record of human improvement according to the believer's conception of the good, and that this improvement may or must continue into the foreseeable future, then it is difficult to resist J.B. Bury's contention that the belief in progress did not really arrive in Western thought until the eighteenth-century Enlightenment.[3]

[2] Christopher Dawson, *Progress and Religion*, Garden City, N.Y., Image Books, 1960, pp. 7–8.

[3] See J. B. Bury, *The Idea of Progress*, New York, Macmillan, 1932, especially Chapters V–VI.

Medieval Christian thought had of course advanced the belief that the human race (or part of it) would enjoy celestial bliss in a miraculous "future" outside of time; but this was not an idea of progress within history, although a few millenarian prophets such as Joachim of Floris seem to have anticipated a type of heaven on earth, destined to precede the Second Coming of Christ and the true end of time. Nor can one discover ideas of progress as defined above in the thought of the Renaissance or the seventeenth-century philosophers. A conception of the progress of technology and knowledge emerged between 1450 and 1700 which, no doubt, profoundly influenced later thought, but which still fell short of an idea of general progress.

At the same time, it is certainly arguable that the early modern view of man as a creative force in history, coupled with the belief that the "moderns" were quite the equals of the "ancients," constitutes the germ of the later, full-blown doctrines of general human progress. For this reason, the present volume includes selections from the works of Jean Bodin and Bernard le Bovier de Fontenelle.

The anthology continues with representative excerpts from the thought of such authentic exponents of progress as Immanuel Kant, the Marquis de Condorcet, Auguste Comte, Karl Marx, and T.H. Huxley. In the last two parts, the faith in progress comes under attack from Jacob Burckhardt and Reinhold Niebuhr and is at least partially reaffirmed by Arnold J. Toynbee.

Several articles and excerpts illustrative of recent scholarly thinking on the idea of progress are also included. But this literature has never been extensive, and surprisingly little dispassionate discussion is available of the broad interpretative issues involved. "Progress" is not a fact or an observable phenomenon, but a judgment of value, which must be made on the basis of a survey of the total achievement of the human race in historical time. Such judgments are both easy and impossible to make: easy because most people have a certain intuitive feeling about the meaning of history, and impossible because no one has enough knowledge or wisdom to take the measure of the totality of human experience in a manner satisfactory to the demands of science.

In any event, not many scholars dealing with the problem can refrain from interposing their own feelings about progress, so that the conventional line between the "primary" and the "secondary" source becomes difficult sometimes to draw. Most of the "secondary" authorities excerpted in this anthology have made their own value judgments quite obvious, while, at the same time, many of the "primary" sources offer us a good deal of purely scholarly insight into the problems at hand. It should also be recalled that such prophets of progress as Comte and Marx believed quite seriously that they were enunciating, as social scientists, laws of progress. In their own view of the matter, judgments of value had little to do with it, although most Western thinkers today would be unwilling to accept them as objective scholars.

At least four major interpretative problems can be distinguished in the study of the idea of progress, and the reader will find them discussed at a number of points in the texts that follow.

The first is the problem of whether progress itself has occurred and will continue to occur: a problem that might conceivably fall within the jurisdiction of the philosopher, the anthropologist, the sociologist, or the historian. The second is the problem of whether it is possible to discern "laws" of progress. No doubt, the philosopher is most competent to answer this question. Unlike the first, it can be answered without making normative assertions.

A third problem is the issue of the origins and development of the belief in progress. When did it first arise? What material conditions and what traditions in thought may have had some influence on its early growth? What stages can be distinguished in its evolution through the centuries? What influence has it had on the Western spirit, and has it fallen in the twentieth century into decline? These are questions for the intellectual historian to answer and, again, they can be answered without resort to normative assertions, although in practice this may be difficult to do.

Finally, there is the problem of defining what we mean by "progress." None of the other problems can be approached rationally without a complete working definition of the term, but much of the literature on the idea of progress fails to supply its readers with such a definition or, if it does, fails to use it consistently. As a result, many of the alleged differences of view between both prophets and scholars reduce to semantic differences. What one thinker means by progress is not at all what another means by it. Confusion of the worst sort is inevitable. The reader is invited as he works along in this anthology to take special note of the various ways in which the terms "progress" and "idea of progress" are employed.

PART ONE

Definitions and Origins

1 Carl L. Becker

Carl L. Becker (1873-1945) was one of America's most gifted intellectual historians. His Heavenly City of the Eighteenth-Century Philosophers (1932) remains, more than a third of a century later, the best short study of the French Enlightenment. In the article that follows, Becker presents a brief history of the belief in progress, seasoned with his own rather melancholy reflections on the relativity of world views. Notice his emphasis on the organic relationship between Christian faith and modern ideas of progress.

"Thought," says Pascal, "makes the greatness of man." The universe can destroy an individual by a mere breath; but even if the entire force of the universe were employed to destroy a single man, the man "would still be more noble than that which destroys him, since he is aware of his own death and of the advantage which the universe has over him: of all this the universe knows nothing." This awareness of himself and of the universe is no doubt what chiefly distinguishes man from all other forms of life. Man alone is conscious in the sense that he alone can stand outside of himself, as it were, and watch himself functioning for a brief span in the universe of which he is part. Man alone can coordinate memory of things past, perception of things present, anticipation of things to come, sufficiently so at least to know that he, like generations before him and after him, will live his brief span and will die. It is in virtue of this awareness, and somewhat in proportion to its intensity, that man alone asks the fundamental questions. Why and for what purpose this brief and precarious existence in a universe that endures? What is man's relation to the universe that is sometimes friendly, sometimes hostile, but in the

SOURCE. Carl L. Becker, "Progress," in *Encyclopedia of the Social Sciences*, New York: Macmillan, 1934, XII, pp. 495–499. Reprinted with permission of The Macmillan Company from *Encyclopedia of the Social Sciences*, edited by Seligman and Johnson. Copyright 1934 by The Macmillan Company, renewed 1962 by The Macmillan Company.

end always fatal to him? How may he elude its hostility, win its favor, find compensations for the intolerable certainty of the death which it will inflict upon him? The answers which men have given to these questions are to be found in the various myths, religious doctrines, philosophical and ethical interpretations which they have accepted, and in those unconsciously held preconceptions which in every age so largely shape their thought and conduct. The modern idea of progress belongs in this category of answers to necessary but insoluble questions. Like the myths of primitive peoples and the religious and philosophical beliefs of more advanced societies, it springs from the nature of man as a conscious creature, who finds existence intolerable unless he can enlarge and enrich his otherwise futile activities by relating them to something more enduring and significant than himself.

Although grounded in the nature of man as a conscious creature, the idea of progress belongs historically to the European tradition, and its origin may be derived from two sources. One of these is the classical conception of history as an endless series of cycles; the other is the Hebraic-Christian doctrine of messianic intervention and salvation.

In Greek mythology the reign of Cronus was regarded as a golden age when men lived like gods free from toil and grief. The present appeared to be a period of degeneration, and improvement or progress could be conceived only in terms of regeneration—a return to the lost golden age. After the myth ceased to be believed, the Greeks continued to look back to the time of great lawgivers, such as Lycurgus and Solon, whose work they idealized, and forward to the time when other great lawgivers would appear and give them better laws again. "Until philosophers become kings . . . ," said Plato, "cities will not cease from ill." Yet however often restoration was accomplished by inspired lawgivers of philosopher-kings, fate and human frailty would again bring degeneration; so that, since "time is the enemy of man," most classical writers regarded human history as an endless series of cycles, a continual repetition of the familiar phenomena of recovery and degeneration. The rational mind, according to Marcus Aurelius, "stretches forth into the infinitude of Time, and comprehends the cyclical Regeneration of all things, and . . . discerns that our children will see nothing fresh, just as our fathers too never saw anything more than we" (*The Communings with Himself of Marcus Aurelius Antoninus*, tr. by C. R. Haines, Loeb Classical Library, London 1916, bk. xi, sect. 1). To regenerate the Roman Empire was obviously less easy than to construct a constitution for a small city-state; and Marcus Aurelius, philosopher-king though he was, instead of giving new laws to society recommended that the individual cultivate resignation. The later centuries of the Roman Empire, when resignation became at once more necessary and more difficult, were therefore a suitable time for the hopeless classical doctrine of endless cycles to be replaced by the Hebraic-Christian doctrine of messianic intervention and salvation.

The Jews like the Greeks looked back to a golden age, but it was identified with the creation of the world and with the Garden of Eden, in which the first men lived in innocence. Like the Greeks the Jews regarded the present as a period of degeneration, but they attributed the "fall" to Adam's disobedience to God's commands. God was at once the omniscient creator of the world and the supreme lawgiver, so that regeneration was identified with the coming of a God inspired king of the house of David. Multiplied reverses and the destruction of the Hebraic state gave to this doctrine a less political, a more mystical and transcendent character. The once actual but now vanished kingdom was replaced by an ideal Israel, symbolized as the "son of man"; and the idea of a God inspired king was replaced by the idea of a messiah who would effect a catastrophic intervention in the affairs of men and pronounce a doomlike judgment on the world. The Christian myth was but an elaboration of these ideas. Jesus, son of man, son of God, was the Messiah. But the end was not yet. The death of Jesus was expiation for the sins of men, faith in Him the means of salvation. Jesus the man was dead, but Christ the Lord still lived and would come again; then the earthly city would be destroyed and all the faithful be gathered with God in the heavenly city, there to dwell in perfection forever.

The weakness of the classical version of degeneration and recovery was that it offered no ultimate hope; of the Jewish, that its promise was for the chosen people only. The strength of the Christian version was that, conceiving human history as a cosmic drama in which all men played their predestined part, it offered to all the hope of eternal life as a compensation for the frustrations of temporal existence: by transferring the golden age from the past to the future it substituted an optimistic for a disillusioned view of human destiny. It is easily to be understood that such a view won wide assent in the Roman Empire during the centuries (300–500) of declining prosperity and increasing oppression or that it served so well to make existence tolerable in the relatively anarchic, isolated and static society of western Europe from the dissolution of the Roman Empire to the Renaissance of classical learning. But it lost its hold on the imaginations of men as a result of profound changes in the outward conditions of life which occurred in western Europe from the fourteenth to the nineteenth century. Among these changes were the rise of ordered secular governments, the growth of towns and industry, the geographical discoveries and the extension of commerce which brought western Europe into direct contact with alien customs and ideas, and above all the rise of an educated middle class whose interests were hampered by a form of society in which both the power and the doctrines of the Christian church supported the autocracy of kings and the privileges of a landed aristocracy. It was in this time of revolt against ecclesiastical and secular authority that the Christian doctrine of salvation was gradually transformed into the modern idea of progress.

So long as Christian philosophy was little questioned, men could afford to ignore the factual experience of mankind since they were so well assured of its ultimate significance. But the declining influence of the church was accompanied by an increasing interest in the worldly activities of men in the past. Italian humanists turned to the study of classical writers; Protestant reformers appealed from current theologians to the beliefs and practises of the primitive church. Thus was born the modern historical approach to problems, and human life came increasingly to be regarded rather as a historical process than as a finished drama to be played out according to a divine plan. Seen in historical perspective, classical civilization emerged for the humanists as a resplendent epoch from which the middle period of ecclesiastical ascendancy was manifestly a degeneration. Until the seventeenth century secular thought and learning turned for inspiration to the past—to the golden ages of Pericles and Augustus; and classical writers were idealized as models to be imitated, to be equaled if possible but hardly to be surpassed. In all this there was nothing that could not be found in the Greek notion of history with its cycles of recovery and degeneration, and but for two general influences modern thought might have been no more than a return to the classical view of human destiny.

One of these influences was Christian philosophy itself: Although it was gradually discredited as an account of events historically verifiable, Christian philosophy had so thoroughly habituated men to the thought of an ultimate happy destiny that they could never be content with a pale imitation of Greek pessimism. The other influence was experimental science which, in proportion as it displaced the Christian notion of a utopian existence after death to be brought about by the miraculous intervention of God, opened up the engaging prospect of indefinite improvement in this life to be effected by the application of human reason to the mastery of the physical and social environment which determines men's lives for good or ill.

In the seventeenth century Galileo and Newton made possible a new attitude toward nature. Nature was now seen to be friendly to man since the universe behaved in a uniform way according to universal natural laws—a behavior capable of being observed and measured and subjected to the uses of men. God was still the supreme lawgiver, the author of the universe; but His will was revealed in the great book of nature which men were to study in order to interpret, and to interpret in order that their ideas and customs might attain an increasing perfection by being brought into greater harmony with the laws of nature and of nature's God. God's revelation to men was thus made not through an inspired book or a divinely established church but through His works, and man had been endowed with reason precisely that he might learn through the course of the centuries what that revelation was. It was therefore no longer so necessary to think of the golden age of Greece and Rome as unsurpassable. "Those whom we call the ancients were really those who lived in the youth of the world," said Pascal, and "as we have added the experience of the ages between us and them to what they knew, it is in ourselves that is to be found that antiquity which we venerate in others." In the ascription of antiquity to the race there is still the implication of degeneration; but if a continuously richer experience made the moderns wiser than the ancients, it was not difficult to hit upon the idea that future generations would, in virtue of the same advantages, surpass the moderns, "We have admired our ancestors less," said Chastellux, "but we have loved our contemporaries better, and have expected more of our descendants" (*De la félicité publique*, 2 vols., new ed. Paris 1822, vol. ii, p. 71). Thus in the eighteenth century the modern idea of progress was born. Under the pressure of social discontents the dream of perfection, that necessary compensation for the limitations of the present state, having long been identified with the golden age or the Garden of Eden or life eternal in the heavenly city of God, was at last projected into the temporal life of man on earth and identified with the desired and hoped for regeneration of society.

As formulated by the *philosophes* the doctrine of progress was but a modification, however important, of the Christian doctrine of redemption; what was new in it was faith in the goodness of man and the efficacy of conscious reason to create an earthly utopia. The French Revolution was the outward expression of this faith. In the nineteenth century the doctrine of progress still reigned and won even a wider popular support, but it was somewhat differently conceived. After the disillusionment occasioned by the revolution and the Napoleonic conquests the prevailing desire was for social stability and national independence. The rationalization of this desire was provided by the historians and jurists who formulated the notion of historical continuity and deprecated the attempt to transform institutions according to a rational plan. Change was considered necessary but was thought to be beneficial only when it issued spontaneously from national tradition; the concept of natural law was not abandoned, but it was regarded as implicit in historical evolution rather than as a conclusion from abstract reason. Law is not made by the legislator, said Savigny, any more than language is made by the grammarian. Ranke, who influenced three generations of historians, viewed progress as something to be discovered by tracing the history of each nation just as it had occurred and by noting the peculiar contribution which each nation at the appropriate moment had made to European civilization. Hegel formulated the point of view of early nineteenth century jurists and historians in his *Philosophie der Geschichte*. A reason of nature working over the heads of men, a transcendent *Vernunft* reconciling within its cloudy recesses innumerable and conflicting *Verstände*, progressively realized itself in the actual events of history.

After the middle of the century natural science invested the doctrine of progress with a more materialistic implication. Progress was still regarded as the result of a force external to man; but the force was to be found not above but inherent in the phenomenal world. This view found support in the Darwinian theory of struggle for existence and survival of the fittest and in Schopenhauer's doctrine of the will as an aspect of a universal blind force. Guided by these preconceptions thinkers abandoned the effort to hasten progress by describing utopias and turned to the search for the inevitable law by which progress had been and would be achieved. Of the many efforts of this sort the most important were those of Auguste Comte and Karl Marx. Comte looked upon history as the result of the instinctive effort of men to ameliorate their condition—an effort which could be observed to fall into three stages of culture, the theological, the metaphysical and the positive, or scientific. Marx, interpreting the historic process in terms of Hegel's famous dialectic, found the determining force in the economic class conflict which, having substituted the nineteenth century capitalist competitive society for the aristocratic landed society of the Middle Ages and early modern times, would in turn replace the capitalist competitive society of the nineteenth century by the proletarian communist society of the future.

Of the many theories of progress formulated in the nineteenth century the only one that had much influence on the thought of common men was that of Marx. Yet the idea of progress, vaguely conceived as a rapid improvement in general prosperity and happiness, became a living force. The chief reason for this was no doubt the rapid changes in the outward conditions of life consequent upon the technological revolution. The common man, before whose eyes the marvels of science and invention were constantly displayed, noted the unprecedented increase in wealth, the growth of cities, the new and improved methods of transportation and communication, the greater security from disease and death and all the conveniences of domestic life unknown to previous generations, and accepted the doctrine of progress without question: the world was obviously better than it had been, obviously would be better than it was. The precise objective toward which the world was progressing remained, however, for the common man and for the intellectual, somewhat vague.

Thus the nineteenth century doctrine of progress differed somewhat from that of the eighteenth. The difference may be expressed, with some exaggeration in the contrast, by saying that whereas the eighteenth century held that man can by taking thought add a cubit to his stature, the nineteenth century held that a cubit would be added to his stature whether he took thought or not. This latter faith that the stars were carrying men on to better things received a rude shock during the World War and subsequently; and there may be noted two significant changes in the present attitude toward the doctrine of progress. Certain thinkers, notably Spengler, are returning to the Greek notion of cycles, now formulated in terms of the rise, flourishing and decline of "cultures." Others are reverting to the eighteenth century idea that by deliberate purpose and the rational use of knowledge man can reconstruct society according to a more just and intelligible design. To this class belong those who have faith in communism, fascism and the planned capitalist society.

The doctrine of progress is peculiarly suited to western society in modern times; that is, a highly dynamic society capable of seeing its achievements against a long historical background. From the practical and from the rational point of view there is no reason to suppose that it will have a more enduring virtue than other doctrines which it has supplanted. If, as may well happen, the possibilities of scientific discovery and of technological invention should sometime be exhausted, the outward conditions of life might become sufficiently stabilized so that the idea of progress would cease to be relevant. Rationally considered, the idea of progress is always at war with its premises. It rests upon the notion of a universe in perpetual flux; yet the idea of progress has always carried the implication of finality, for it seems to be meaningless unless there is movement toward some ultimate objective. The formal theories of progress are all vitiated by this radical inconsistency. In Hegel's scheme the objective was freedom, already realized in the Prussian state. In Comte's theory the objective was the final positive stage into which Europe had already entered. Marx criticized Hegel for explaining history by a process which would not explain the future, but he is himself open to the criticism of having explained history in terms of a class conflict which would end with the establishment of a classless society. It is easy to picture history as a process working toward an ultimate good if the world is to come to an end when that good is attained; but if the universe as presented by modern science is to be accepted —a universe in perpetual flux—then a law of history which at some determinate time ceases to apply leaves much to be desired.

Thus the final good, absolute standards of value, are sought in vain; there is merely a universe in which the ideas of things as well as the things themselves arise out of temporary conditions and are transformed with the modification of the conditions out of which they arose. On this assumption we must dispense with the notion of finality, must suppose that the idea of progress and all of its special formulations are but temporary insights useful for the brief moment in which they flourish. "In escaping from the illusion of finality, is it legitimate to exempt that dogma itself? Must not it, too, submit to its own negation of finality? Will not that process of change, for which Progress is the optimistic name, compel 'Progress' too to fall from the commanding position in which it is now, with apparent security, enthroned?" (Bury, J. B., *The Idea of Progress*, p. 352). The price we pay for escaping from the illusion of finality is the recognition that nothing, not even the belief that we have escaped that illusion, is likely to endure. All philosophies based upon the absolute and the unconditioned have their defects; but all philosophies based upon the universal relativity of things have their defects also, a minor one being that they must be prepared, at the appropriate moment, to commit hara-kiri in deference to the ceaseless change which they postulate.

Belief in progress as a fact depends upon the standard of value chosen for measuring it and upon the time perspective in which it is measured. If we look back a hundred years, it is obvious that there has been progress in the mastery of physical forces. If we look back two thousand years, it is uncertain whether there has been much if any progress in intelligence and the art of living. If we look back two hundred and fifty thousand years, it is apparent that there has been progress in all those aspects of life which civilized men regard as valuable. All these judgments are based on standards of value appreciable by the mind of civilized man. But if we take a still longer perspective and estimate the universe as a whole, as an omniscient intelligence indifferent to human values might estimate it, in terms of cosmic energy, then progress and the very existence of man himself become negligible and meaningless. In such a perspective we should see the whole life of man on the earth as a mere momentary ripple on the surface of one of the minor planets in one of the minor stellar systems.

2 W. Warren Wagar

Becker's attention to the Jewish and Christian roots of the belief in progress is typical of contemporary students of the philosophy of history, but other points of view are possible, as may be seen in this article from The Journal of the History of Ideas.

In common with other scholars in the *Geisteswissenschaften* [cultural sciences], historians of ideas tend to reflect the prevailing values of their own era. One obvious example of this tendency may be found in the abundant scholarly literature on the history of the idea of progress, and above all in the recent shift of opinion

SOURCE. W. Warren Wagar, "Modern Views of the Origins of the Idea of Progress," in *Journal of the History of Ideas*, XXVIII, January-March, 1967, pp. 55–70. Reprinted by permission of the *Journal of the History of Ideas*. Copyright, 1967 by Journal of the History of Ideas, Inc.

from the older view that the idea of progress is a peculiarly modern notion to the now orthodox belief that it is merely a "bastard offspring" of the Christian world-outlook.

Clearly, the two views are not in all respects mutually exclusive. Much also depends on what one means by the idea of progress. Progress in the morally neutral sense of "forward movement" or in the popular sense of advances in technology, need not concern us here. But if progress is taken to mean the gradual betterment of humanity, the difficulty arises that historians vary almost as profoundly in their ideas of what constitutes human betterment as the philosophers of history whose thought they have studied. Only the broadest sort of definition, such as the one offered by Lovejoy and Boas in their *Primitivism and Related Ideas in Antiquity*, will cover all the ground involved. In the discussion which follows, then, the idea of progress is the view that "the course of things since the beginning—in spite of possible minor deviations and the occasional occurrence of backwaters in the stream of history—has been characterized by a gradual progressive increase, or a wider diffusion, of goodness, or happiness, or enlightenment, or of all of these."[1] At the heart of every theory of progress lies a conception of the ultimate good, and progress is thought to occur in proportion as the ultimate good triumphs in history.

Most XIXth-century social prophets and scholars conceived of the idea of progress as a product of the modern spirit. Following Turgot, Kant, and Hegel, they agreed that man had advanced

---

[1] Arthur O. Lovejoy and George Boas, eds., *Primitivism and Related Ideas in Antiquity* (Baltimore, 1935), "Prolegomena to the History of Primitivism," 3. The same writers also identify a "theory of successive progress and decline," which holds that progress has occurred, but that the upward movement of history has already ended, or is ending, or will eventually end, to be followed by decline. *Ibid.,* 4. Where decline is thought to have set in long ago, a theory of successive progress and decline is often confused with chronological primitivism. By the same token, where decline is thought to be recent or scheduled for some future epoch, such a theory is easily mistaken for the idea of continuous progress. Many alleged discoveries of the idea of progress in antiquity or the Renaissance fall into this error, and even such champions of the progressive faith in recent generations as Herbert Spencer actually belong in the camp of the theorists of successive progress and decline.

steadily since the earliest times; but he had not become aware of progress as the grand design of history until the XVIIth or XVIIIth centuries. The magisterial pronouncements of Comte in the *Cours de philosophie positive* found wide acceptance. The ancients, he wrote, looked on order and progress as antithetical principles, and chose order. As for Christianity, "it certainly bore a part in originating the sentiment of social progress by proclaiming the superiority of the new law to the old." But "the theological polity, proceeding upon an immutable type, which was realized only in the past, must have become radically incompatible with ideas of continuous progression, and manifests, on the contrary, a thoroughly retrograde character." The metaphysical era in the history of the human spirit, with its sterile dogmatism, had also failed to enunciate a clear concept of progress. Only with the failure of the theological and metaphysical outlooks could the idea of progress take "any general possession of the public mind." The laws of progress could be developed "by the positive philosophy alone."[2] Sociology, the highest science, had only just now —in Comte's own time and partly as a result of his own labors— begun to apply positive methods to the study of man as a social animal; the law of the three stages, the law of progress, was its fundamental organizing principle, first sketched out by Turgot and Condorcet, and perfected by Comte himself. It could not have appeared before modern times.[3]

Comte's philosophy of history gave him no choice but to insist on the modernity of the idea of progress, but many other prominent thinkers of the century arrived at much the same view independently. Charles Renouvier, a profound opponent of positivism and deterministic theories of history in general, traced the modern faith in progress only as far back as Leibniz. "The belief in general and indefinite progress . . . is, in the eyes of every perceptive critic free of the prejudices of our century, something out of all congruence with Christian ideas." From earliest times Christianity

[2] Auguste Comte, *The Positive Philosophy of Auguste Comte*, freely translated and condensed by Harriet Martineau (New York, 1854), II, 3 and 46–47.

[3] *Cf.* the similar views of Comte's contemporary, Pierre Leroux, in *De l'Humanité* (Paris, 1840), I, 138ff.

had fixed its vision on another world; the modern faith envisaged improvement only in time and on earth.[4]

In a seminal essay written in 1892, Ferdinand Brunetière, another great French savant outside the positivist circle, detected vague anticipations of the idea of progress in antiquity. One could find hints of the idea in *Genesis*, among the ancient Indians, in the philosophy of Epicurus, in early Christianity. Jesus proposed a kind of spiritual progress in declaring the superiority of his revelation to all its predecessors. But none of these were true ideas of progress. "Glimpsed by some, even roughly sketched out by others, [the idea of progress] had no philosophical existence until the eighteenth century. Men caught a glimpse, rather than formed a conception, of it. It floated in the air without anyone having tried to take possession of it."[5] The turning point came with the Battle of the Books in the late XVIIth century, after which the idea passed into general currency during the Enlightenment.

A line of argument similar to Brunetière's was pursued by Robert Flint in his still frequently cited studies of the history of philosophy of history. Since philosophy of history dealt in large measure with laws of progress or evolution, little could have been done in the field "until the idea of progress was firmly and clearly apprehended." But Flint found no such apprehension in ancient medieval thought; it followed that philosophy of history could have had little chance to develop until modern times, which was, in fact, the case. The Greeks and Romans had toyed with the notion of progress, but they had also conceived of history in other ways, "although in none profoundly or consistently." It was not otherwise with Christian thought. Early Christianity had put forward the idea of the spiritual education of humanity by God, but, as formulated by Augustine, the Christian view of history represented "the kingdom of the devil as not less enduring and more populous than that of God, so that the ultimate goal of history is for the majority of human souls one of eternal sin and

[4] Charles Renouvier, *Philosophie analytique de l'histoire* (Paris, 1896–97), III, 359. See also Renouvier's *Introduction à la philosophie analytique de l'histoire*, rev. ed. (Paris, 1896), 555.
[5] Ferdinand Brunetière, *Etudes critiques sur l'histoire de la littérature française*, 5e Série (Paris, 1911), 186.

suffering." In appearance Augustine's theory affirmed the unity and progress of humanity, but to some degree it implicitly denied both. With their "abounding ignorance" and "anarchy," the Middle Ages had also been unfavorable in Flint's judgment to the development of any idea of progress, despite the bold conceptions of such relatively isolated figures as Roger Bacon and Joachim of Floris. It was only with the Renaissance "that the idea of progress could enter into the stage of development in which its significance in all departments of science and existence has gradually come to be recognised."[6]

Curiously enough, the two most ambitious efforts to write the history of the idea of progress before Bury, took an apparently different tack, arguing that the idea had enjoyed a long and venerable history, and had flourished in some form in all the major Western cultures. But in both instances, the author's purpose was more to show the relative modernity of certain currents of premodern thought than to demonstrate, as scholars nowadays are wont to do, the extent to which modern ideas descend, often "illegitimately," from older ideas.

The earlier of these studies was the work of the Belgian sociologist Guillaume De Greef, himself an apostle of progress deeply in the debt of Comte, although he had to oppose the Master on this particular point. He began by attacking "the superficial observation that one encounters in nearly all the writings of those who have concerned themselves with the question," the observation that the idea of progress belongs only to the last few centuries. The first scientific ideas of progress, to be sure, were the work of Turgot, Condorcet, and Comte. But their thought grew in turn out of such fundamental conceptions as the Golden Age, organic evolution, the continuity and regularity of the cosmos, and Jesus' prophecy of the gradual coming of the Kingdom of Heaven, all conceptions which had arisen in antiquity. Like progress itself, the idea of progress had passed through a number of well-defined stages, each one indispensable to those that followed. At no point in ancient or medieval times had the idea of progress succeeded

---

[6] Robert Flint, *History of the Philosophy of History* (New York, 1894), 88, 90, 158, and 104.

in fully emancipating itself from the superstition, pessimism, and tendency to otherworldliness which hampered all premodern thought, but it constantly struggled for existence, growing by degrees from the first faint conceptions of future life in the pre-historic mind to the full-bloom scientific laws of XIXth-century sociology.[7]

A still more elaborate effort to push the idea of progress back into antiquity was made by Jules Delvaille in his encyclopedic *Essai sur l'histoire de l'idée de progrès jusqu'à la fin du XVIIIe siècle*, which remains today the longest book on the subject, though certainly not the best. Bury learned much from it, even if he dissented crucially on the point here at issue. Whereas De Greef had discovered only the germ or embryo of the modern conception of progress in ancient thought, Delvaille seemed to find the thing itself. The proclamation of the Messiah in prophetic Judaism was nothing less than "faith in progress"; the Epicurean theory of progress was a rough draft of Condorcet's *Esquisse;* and so forth.[8] Jesus, Augustine, Joachim, and Roger Bacon received special attention among Christian thinkers. Even more clearly than in the case of De Greef, however, Delvaille's purpose was to point out the pleasantly surprising new-fashionedness of antiquity and not the old-fashionedness of modernity.[9]

[7] Guillaume De Greef, *Le Transformisme social: Essai sur le progrès et le regrès des sociétés* (Paris, 1895). The account of the history of the idea of progress may be found on pp. 8–306.

[8] Jules Delvaille, *Essai sur l'histoire de l'idée de progrès jusqu'à la fin du XVIIIe siècle* (Paris, 1910), 16 and 75.

[9] An interesting parallel might be drawn with some of the theologians of the "Social Gospel," who discovered the modern idea of progress almost intact in the teachings of Jesus. See, for example, Walter Rauschenbusch, *Christianity and the Social Crisis* (New York, 1908), chs. 1–3. In a very different vein, scholars more recently have called attention to the "party of progress" which grew up within the Church in the IVth century, and whose leaders included the historian Eusebius, St. Ambrose, and the poet Prudentius. See E. K. Rand, *Founders of the Middle Ages* (Cambridge, Mass., 1928), 13–22; and Theodor E. Mommsen, "St. Augustine and the Christian Idea of Progress," JHI, XII (1951), 356–69. Mommsen suggests that Augustine wrote *The City of God* in large part to refute the arguments of these too-worldly Christians, who saw the progress of imperial Rome as proof of God's satisfaction with mankind and with Holy Church. *Cf.*

But the majority of scholars down to the appearance of Bury's *magnum opus* in 1920 continued to emphasize the relative novelty of the progressive faith. Ernst Troeltsch noted the unwitting contribution of the Reformers to the modern belief in progress in his lectures on *Protestantism and Progress*, but made quite clear that the belief itself "was an accompanying phenomenon of the struggle for freedom in the period of Illuminism."[10] Arthur J. Todd in *Theories of Social Progress* saw the faith in progress as a child of modern science. "Both the word and the idea . . . are relatively new."[11] Even Dean Inge in his famous 1920 Romanes lecture ruled out any organic connection between classical or Christian thought and the belief in progress. Classical theory of history was fundamentally cyclical, and Christians, Roman and medieval alike, had set their hopes on another world, quite content to see man's career on earth end in their own time. The doctrine of progress had XVIIth-century roots and became widespread, Inge wrote, only in the latter part of the XVIIIth century.[12]

It was certainly Bury's book, however, that did the most to establish the idea of progress as a uniquely modern faith. He began by defining his terms so narrowly that it would have been difficult for a thinker of his outlook to arrive at any other conclusion regarding the origins of the idea of progress. "This idea means that civilisation has moved, is moving, and will move in a desirable direction." In Bury's definition, the forward motion of civilization also had to be thought of as gradual and as destined to continue indefinitely, and it had to be "the necessary outcome of the psychical and social nature of man; it must not be at the mercy of any external will; otherwise there would be no guarantee of its continuance and its issue, and the idea of Progress would lapse into the idea of Providence."[13] So defined, the idea

---

Arthur O. Lovejoy's discussion of the progressivism of Tertullian in " 'Nature' as Norm in Tertullian," *Essays in the History of Ideas* (Baltimore, 1948), 318-22 and 338.

[10] Ernst Troeltsch, *Protestantism and Progress* (London, 1912), 25.

[11] Arthur J. Todd, *Theories of Social Progress* (New York, 1918), 93.

[12] W. R. Inge, *The Idea of Progress* (Oxford, 1920), 3-7.

[13] J. B. Bury, *The Idea of Progress* (New York, 1932), 3-5. (1st ed., London, 1920).

of progress had had no existence before modern times. Classical thought insisted on the unchangeability of human nature and of the ideal world; the historical process was almost invariably thought of as cyclical and in any case no fundamental change in the order of reality was involved. Christian thinkers for their part subjected everything to the will of divine providence and took no real interest in the prospect of terrestrial improvement. Christianity did break the grip of cyclical conceptions of history on the human imagination, and in this sense prepared the way for the theory of progress, but before the possible emergence of anything like a true idea of progress, three other developments had to take place: the authority of the ancients had to be challenged and thought liberated from its yoke; the value of secular life had to be frankly acknowledged; and science had to be put on sure foundations by Descartes' demonstration of the invariability of the laws of nature. All of this happened in the XVIth and XVIIth centuries. By the early XVIIIth century, Western civilization was ready for its first theory of general progress, enunciated by the Abbé de Saint-Pierre.[14]

Bury's severely limited definition of the idea of progress gave to his work less historical scope than it might otherwise have had, but his skill in demolishing the too optimistic interpretations of classical historical thought of some of his precursors should not be underestimated, and if his treatment of Christian thinkers seems rather less convincing, and grounded in less careful research, it is still worth serious consideration. One thing is clear. His book became almost immediately the undisputed classic in its field, comparable in influence to Burckhardt's *Civilization of the Renaissance in Italy* in Renaissance studies. A whole generation of intellectual historians was nourished on Bury, not only because he had produced a brilliant history of an important tradition in thought, but also because he was one of the first scholars writing in English to make generous use of the basic concepts and methods of intellectual history. The standard works on the Scientific Revolution and the Enlightenment of the 1920's and 1930's usually refer to him; most agree with him that the idea of progress was quintes-

---

[14] *Ibid.*, 1–36 and 65–66. For St.-Pierre, see ch. 6.

sentially a modern faith, fathered by modern science.[15] An orthodox position had clearly crystallized. It was a position which, in
the main, looked favorably on the modern world and the modern
spirit, especially as contrasted with the spirit of the Middle Ages.
Most of its exponents were also themselves adherents of the faith
in progress, even if they objected, as did Renouvier, to certain
forms taken by that faith.[16] The same generalizations apply to
those, like De Greef and Delvaille, who preferred to find significant anticipations of the modern spirit in earlier ages.

But in the last twenty or thirty years, a new orthodox position
has emerged which makes Bury suddenly seem old-fashioned and
even quaint in the eyes of many scholars. In part, the development of this new orthodoxy must be ascribed to purely internal
developments in historiography: the natural tendency of younger
generations of scholars to challenge the settled convictions of
older generations, and in particular that powerful movement in
recent historiographical thinking which takes for its motto, "It
happened later than you think, and even then it was little more

[15] See, e.g., Kingsley Martin, *French Liberal Thought in the Eighteenth
Century* (London, 1929), 277–81; and Preserved Smith, *A History of Modern Culture* (New York, 1930–34), II, 228–29. "No psychological contrast
between the older and the more recent thought is of greater consequence
than is the contrast between the backward-looking and the forward-looking
mind. The ancients regarded primitive times as the last age of gold; the
medievals esteemed almost all previous periods as happier than their own.
The humanist of the Renaissance longed for a return to the age of Augustus
and the Reformer sought to restore the purity of the apostolic era. But,
beginning in the seventeenth century, men began to look forward and not
back, to the future and not to the past, for the era of perfection. The reason
for this is simply the triumph of science." Smith, *ibid.* See also Vincent
Brome, *The Problem of Progress* (London, 1963), ch. 1, for a recent example of Bury's continuing influence outside academic circles.

[16] Bury was enough influenced by the relativistic implications of historicism to suggest that the faith in progress would some day be replaced
by another ruling idea, just as progress itself had taken the place of providence. But in so doing, he contradicted himself by retaining a progressive
interpretation of the development of human thought: "In other words, does
not Progress itself suggest that its value as a doctrine is only relative, corresponding to a certain not very advanced stage of civilization; just as
Providence, in its day, was an idea of relative value, corresponding to a stage
somewhat less advanced?" *The Idea of Progress*, 352.

than old wine in new bottles." We learn that the Renaissance and Reformation were not really modern, the Scientific and Industrial and French Revolutions were not really revolutionary, the middle classes were not ascendant in British politics until the XXth century, and the spirit of the Enlightenment was only the spirit of the Middle Ages fitted out with a new vocabulary. By the same token, Marx was only a reincarnated Hebrew prophet, Freud a teacher of the ancient truth of original sin (or alternatively, a child of the Enlightenment), and Einstein a "classical" physicist in the tradition of Aristotle and Newton. But the new orthodoxy on the problem of the origins of the idea of progress strikes more fundamentally at the old orthodoxy than would a mere change in historiographical fashions. It reflects the actual collapse of the progressive faith which has taken place by degrees over the past fifty years and the new seriousness with which religion, and the great traditions of religious thought, are being taken by intellectuals, who see in those traditions a radical answer to the spiritual problems of modern man. The new orthodoxy, much of it the result of the impressive work of Christian scholars, rejects not only the assumption that the idea of progress is a uniquely modern faith. It also implicitly or explicitly rejects the idea of progress itself, along with most of the other so-called modern articles of faith with which it was closely associated in the XVIIIth and XIXth centuries: belief in the essential goodness and self-sufficiency of man and faith in the power of science to banish suffering and bring about the "evanescence of evil."

Some of the first and best blows were struck by Carl Becker in his *Heavenly City of the Eighteenth-Century Philosophers*. Although anything but an apologist for Christianity, Becker wrote his *Heavenly City*, as Leo Gershoy points out, in a mood of disillusionment. He had come to the bleak conclusion that the XVIIIth-century religion of humanity "was as little—or as much —tenable as the orthodox Christianity which it had supplanted."[17] It was not only as little tenable; it sprang, as one could determine from an authentically *geisteswissenschaftliche* investigation into

[17] Leo Gershoy in Raymond O. Rockwood, ed., *Carl Becker's Heavenly City Revisited* (Ithaca, N.Y., 1958), 197.

its spiritual sources, from the same thought-world. Becker devoted his fourth chapter, "The Uses of Posterity," to an extensive comparison of the Christian and Enlightenment views of human destiny. The *philosophes* had had no choice, he suggested, but to find a dream just as intoxicating as the Christian dream which they could not accept. If they were to win the common man, in particular, they had to match the Christians promise for promise. "Without a new heaven to replace the old, a new way of salvation, of attaining perfection, the religion of humanity would appeal in vain to the common run of men."[18] In place of a heaven outside of time, the *philosophes* offered the idea of the perfectibility of man on earth. In place of providence and the atonement, they offered the concerted efforts of mankind itself. In place of the judgment of God, they offered the opinion of posterity. The same feelings, the same hopes, the same yearnings were called forth as in the apparently discredited faith of the Middle Ages, for the simple reason that the *philosophes* were not far removed in spirit and purpose from their medieval forerunners. Becker put his case rather more succinctly in his article on progress in the *Encyclopaedia of the Social Sciences*. The modern idea of progress, he wrote, grew out of the Judeo-Christian tradition of messianic intervention and salvation under the stimulus of the hopes raised by modern science. "As formulated by the *philosophes*, the doctrine of progress was but a modification, however important, of the Christian doctrine of redemption; what was new in it was faith in the goodness of man and the efficacy of conscious reason to create an earthly utopia."[19]

In perspective, Becker's argument appears as a sort of prolegomenon to the massive assault on the idea of progress and on Bury's interpretation of its origins which was launched by a number of Christian theologians and devout lay scholars especially in the years just after World War II, and which has resulted in the establishment of what I have called the new orthodox position on the origins of the progressive faith. Becker was not alone in herald-

[18] Carl Becker, *The Heavenly City of the Eighteenth-Century Philosophers* (New Haven, Conn., 1932), 129.

[19] Becker, "Progress," *Encyclopaedia of the Social Sciences*, XII (1934), 497.

ing this assault. Even before *The Heavenly City*, Christopher Dawson, for example, had made much the same case for the origins of the idea of progress in his *Progress and Religion*, going even further to maintain that such spiritual vitality as the idea possessed it drew directly from "the Christian teleological conception of life."[20] But Dawson's observations, like Becker's, could do little more than reopen the question answered with such apparent authority by Bury. Neither book had mounted anything like a full-scale attack.

The postwar attack has been the work primarily of five thinkers, all of them in the front rank, and all worthy opponents of Bury: Karl Löwith in *Meaning in History*, Reinhold Niebuhr in *Faith and History*, John Baillie in *The Belief in Progress*, Eric Voegelin in *The New Science of Politics*, and Emil Brunner in *Eternal Hope*. Other books by these and other scholars might also be cited, but these five give a full statement of the new thinking. The themes more or less common to all of them are easily summarized. All agree that the modern idea of progress cannot be understood or its history written without the most searching inquiry into the mind of antiquity and the Middle Ages. When such an inquiry is made, it discloses an organic connection between pre-modern and modern conceptions of history, but not, of course, the sort of progressive development traced by De Greef. The place of progressive development is taken by struggle and corruption: the struggle between the pagan and Christian outlooks, followed by the corruption or perversion of the latter into the modern idea of progress, usually with the fateful assistance of Christian perfectionists in the late Middle Ages and Reformation. As Jacques Barzun disposes of Darwin, Marx, and Wagner by claiming to prove that all three were not only wrong and wicked but also highly unoriginal, so the new orthodoxy attempts to demolish the idea of progress by exposing at the same time its errors and its illegitimate origins.

The first plank in the platform of the new orthodoxy is an

[20] C. Dawson, *Progress and Religion* (London, 1929), ch. 8, "The Secularization of Western Culture and the Rise of the Religion of Progress," esp. 190–91; also John Macmurray, *The Clue to History* (London, 1938), 113–15.

insistence upon the radically ahistorical world-view of classical civilization. Classical thought held that all historical processes were cyclical; on the other hand, since essential reality was immune to temporal vicissitudes, history had only the most relative and limited significance. In Niebuhr's words, "the classical culture, elaborated by Plato, Aristotle and the Stoics, is a western and intellectual version of a universal type of ahistorical spirituality. . . . For classical culture the world of change and becoming was intelligible and real insofar as it participated in the changeless world through a cycle of changeless recurrence."[21] The characteristic attitude of classical man was that of the Stoics: resignation, fatalism, non-resistance. The world could be understood, but it could not be fundamentally changed.[22]

Against this conception of time and history early Christianity struggled fiercely, drawing on its Jewish heritage, and in due course its opponents met with total defeat. Augustine's writing of *The City of God* was but one event in that struggle, though perhaps the most decisive. Christianity offered the pagans a hopeful and meaningful conception of history. Weary and despondent, they snatched at it eagerly, and so the spiritual life of mankind was radically transformed. "For the first time in the history of humanity," writes Emil Brunner, "through the instrumentality of Israel, and then through the Christian heirs of the Israelite religion of revelation, it happened that the attention of man was directed towards the future."[23] Time was now thought of as linear, as non-reversible, proceeding from the events in *Genesis* to the axial moment of Christ's crucifixion and resurrection and from that point on to the final consummation at the end of the time-line and of time itself. "It was the Christian faith and not modern culture which overwhelmed the classical world. Long before the modern sense of a dynamic and creative history made

---

[21] Reinhold Niebuhr, *Faith and History* (New York, 1949), 16 and 38.

[22] *Cf.* John Baillie, *The Belief in Progress* (London, 1950), 42–57; Emil Brunner, *Eternal Hope* (Philadelphia, 1954), 15–16 and 46–47; Karl Löwith, *Meaning in History* (Chicago, 1949), 199–200; Eric Voegelin, *The New Science of Politics* (Chicago, 1952), 118–19, and *Order and History* (Baton Rouge, La., 1956–57), II, 49–52.

[23] Brunner, 25.

the classical scheme of meaning dubious, the Christian faith challenged and overwhelmed it."[24]

From these two points, which most contemporary scholars would probably find eminently acceptable, the proponents of the new orthodoxy advance to the assumption that the modern idea of progress, formulated as it was by Christians and ex-Christians in a Christian civilization, is only a rendering in secular concepts of the Christian epic, a direct importation of the teachings of the Church on the subject of sacred history into a post-Christian ideology explaining profane history. The importation is in the nature of a rape. The results are illegitimate, since they pervert the meaning of the original Christian teaching and spring from the unholy union of Christian doctrine with modern Western *hubris*. At least this is Brunner's way of putting the matter. Progressivism, he says, "is the bastard offspring of an optimistic anthropology and Christian eschatology." It could have arisen only in a Christian society. "Belief in progress was only possible in Christian Western Europe, but only because in proportion as Christian faith declined the former arose as its distortion and substitute, its parasite. For it lived on the very powers which it destroyed."[25]

John Baillie delivers a similar indictment in *The Belief in Progress*. The idea of progress arose only in Western civilization because it "could not have grown up elsewhere than on ground prepared for it by the Christian Gospel. So far, therefore, as it

[24] Niebuhr, 65. *Cf.* Baillie, 57–84; Löwith, 160–90; Niebuhr, 20–29, 46–54, and 102–50; and Voegelin, *The New Science of Politics,* 107–10. This severe contrast between the classical and Christian ideas of history is a commonplace of recent scholarship. See, *e.g.,* C. N. Cochrane, *Christianity and Classical Culture* (New York, 1944), 243–45 and 483–85; R. G. Collingwood, *The Idea of History* (Oxford, 1946), 46–49; Oscar Cullmann, *Christ and Time: The Primitive Christian Conception of Time and History* (Philadelphia, 1950), esp. 51–60; Erich Frank, *Philosophical Understanding and Religious Truth* (New York, 1945), 67–70; Paul Tillich, *The Interpretation of History* (New York, 1936), 243–48; and Voegelin, *Order and History,* II, 22–23.

[25] Brunner, *Christianity and Civilization* (New York, 1948–49), I, 55; and *Eternal Hope,* 10. Brunner also recapitulates his argument in his *Dogmatics* (Philadelphia, 1950–62), III, 355–61.

may be considered to be false, the doctrine of progress is a Christian heresy. Like all heresies it is essentially a lopsided growth. It is the development of one aspect of the received truth to the neglect of other aspects." He goes on to attack Bury for not bringing out the "extent to which the idea of progress is itself a derivation, legitimate or not, from Christian conceptions," and praises Becker for arguing that the belief in progress was "essentially a redisposition of the Christian ideas which it seeks to displace."[26] Karl Löwith, showing the intimate connection between all modern philosophy of history and Christian thought, finds that the belief in progress is "a sort of religion, derived from the Christian faith in a future goal, though substituting an indefinite and immanent *eschaton* for a definite and transcendent one." It is "as Christian by derivation as it is anti-Christian by implication and . . . definitely foreign to the thought of the ancients. . . . The eschatological interpretation of secular history in terms of judgment and salvation never entered the minds of ancient historians. It is the remote and yet intense result of Christian hope and Jewish expectation."[27] In studying modern prophets, Löwith has no trouble revealing the man of Jewish or Christian faith under the veneer of atheistic rhetoric. Marx was "a Jew of Old Testament stature," and the idealistic basis of his message was "the old Jewish messianism and prophetism . . . and Jewish insistence on absolute righteousness." Insofar as he preached hope, and looked obsessively into the future, even Nietzsche was little more than a heretic, "not so much 'the last disciple of Dionysos' as the first radical apostate of Christ."[28] Along the same lines, we have Voegelin's thesis of modernity as the "redivinization" of man and society, and Niebuhr's assertion that the modern idea of progress puts history in place of Christ as man's redeemer.[29]

---

[26] Baillie, 95, 106, and 113; see also 186–87.
[27] Löwith, 114 and 61.
[28] *Ibid.*, 44 and 222.
[29] Voegelin, *The New Science of Politics,* 107–10 and 128–32; Niebuhr, viii and 1–2. Niebuhr (209–13) offers much the same explanation of Marx as Löwith. In all fairness, it should be added that Niebuhr's formula for the origins of the idea of progress is somewhat more complex than those of the other writers quoted. In addition to the obvious Judeo-Christian ingredient,

Finally, most of our writers attach special significance to certain medieval heresies and movements in the Protestant Reformation as agencies for the transmission of Christian doctrine to the apostles of the idea of progress during and after the Enlightenment. Voegelin directs most of his fire at Joachim of Floris, who becomes in his treatment the arch-villain of modern history. Joachim's idea of the three ages of history, corresponding to the three persons of the Trinity, broke decisively with the Augustinian doctrine of the two cities and injected into the stream of Western thought the poisonous faith in man's perfectibility on earth which was later more fully immanentized, which is to say secularized, by the *philosophes* of the Enlightenment. Joachitic eschatology must be interpreted as a revival of Gnosticism, and modern civilization is spiritually governed by three secularized products of Joachim's Gnostic dream world: the Enlightenment idea of progress, utopianism, and revolutionary perfectionism, of which the clearest modern example is Marxism. The line of descent from Joachim's third and coming age of human perfection to Comte's age of Positivism, the Marxist vision of the classless society, and the Nazi idea of the Third Reich, could not be more clear. The Joachitic poison had worked potently, for example, in all the many perfectionist sects of the later Middle Ages and the Reformation. Voegelin devotes a whole chapter to one such case: the Puritan program for "Gnostic revolution," which strongly influenced the later course of modern thought in its turn.[30] In all of this, Voegelin closely follows the case against Joachim in Löwith's *Meaning in History;* and related passages may be found in Brunner and Niebuhr. Löwith finds it "one of the great paradoxes in the history of Christianity that the most authentic imitation of Christ, that of St. Francis, merged into a revolutionary interpretation of the 'Eternal Gospel' [Joachim's] which led, by

---

he also suggests a major obligation to the classical idea of "rational intelligibility," applied by modern man to the interpretation of history. The idea of progress is, then, a combination of the classical fondness for simple rational explanation, Christian soteriology and eschatology, and the uniquely modern idea of historical development (14–16, 29–30, 37–38, and 65–69).

[30] Voegelin, *The New Science of Politics,* 110–21 (on Joachim), and 113–61 (on the Puritans).

many detours and perversions, to a progressive interpretation of
history which expected the *eschaton* not only in history but
eventually also from it."[31]

The new orthodoxy has, needless to add, found support in many
other quarters. Rudolf Bultmann, while maintaining in effect that
even the medieval Catholic interpretation of history partook of
heresy, and that Christians must look for the *eschaton* only in
every present moment of their lives, subscribes fully to the theory
that the idea of progress was a secularized form of traditional
Christian eschatological doctrine.[32] Ernest Lee Tuveson's brilliant
monograph on XVIIth-century English millenarian philosophies
of history, *Millennium and Utopia*, studies the religious background of the idea of progress and argues that while Descartes
and Newton may take credit for modern naturalism, modern
man's progressive interpretation of history stemmed from theology. The XVIIIth-century faith in progress "resulted in part
from the transformation of a religious idea—the great millennial
expectation."[33] Charles Frankel and R. V. Sampson have both
pointed out the organic link between the spirit and methods of
medieval philosophy and that aspect of the progressive faith
which descends from Descartes.[34] Frank Manuel urges that the
Enlightenment doctrine of progress was "born in the bosom of
Christianity," dramatically illustrated by the fact that Turgot's
famous lectures on the subject at the Sorbonne were intended as
exercises in Christian apologetics. The faith in progress was a
species of "theodicy."[35]

[31] Löwith, 114; also ch. 8 and Appendix I, "Modern Transfigurations of
Joachism." *Cf.* Brunner, *Eternal Hope*, 70–76; and Niebuhr, 2 and 200–09.
Baillie (191 f.n.) prefers to regard Joachim as a rather crude anticipation of
his own particular variety of Christian progressivism.

[32] Rudolf Bultmann, *History and Eschatology* (Edinburgh, 1957), ch. 5.

[33] Ernest Lee Tuveson, *Millennium and Utopia: A Study in the Background of the Idea of Progress* (Berkeley and Los Angeles, 1949), x.

[34] Charles Frankel, *The Faith of Reason: The Idea of Progress in the
French Enlightenment* (New York, 1948), 13–29 and 153–58; R. V. Sampson, *Progress in the Age of Reason* (Cambridge, Mass., 1956), 13–29.

[35] Frank E. Manuel, *The Prophets of Paris* (Cambridge, Mass., 1962), 45–
51. Although in his latest book he warns against pushing the origins of the
idea of progress too far back into the past, this would seem to be a protest

Nor have the proponents of the new orthodoxy gone entirely unchallenged. A few progressivists have protested, notably—in quite another context—Frankel himself, and also Morris Ginsberg. But Ginsberg's protest is rather feeble, asking only that greater stress be laid once again on the importance of modern science, rationalism, and liberalism in the origins of the progressive faith; and Frankel confines himself to a refutation of Niebuhr's charge that the *philosophes* shared any of the sweeping optimism of Christian soteriology.[36] No really effective counterattack has been made, and the new orthodoxy gains ground every year. Perhaps it deserves to. But clearly the motives of many of the scholars involved are open to suspicion. Have they written, if this is possible, out of a pure desire to understand the origins of the idea of progress, or are they engaged in eloquent partisan polemics? Contemporary man's disillusionment with the progressive faith, which attains sometimes the proportions of fury, inevitably colors any attempt to write the history of that faith. Its still sur-

---

against the Delvaille-De Greef school of thought, and not against the essential insights of the new orthodoxy. Manuel is even dubious of Bury's contention that the idea of progress had arrived in the XVIIIth century; the "full-blown" theory of all-inclusive, inevitable, infinite progress did not in his reckoning make its appearance until the early XIXth century and Comte. Manuel, *Shapes of Philosophical History* (Stanford, Calif., 1965), 68–69.

[36] Morris Ginsberg, "The Idea of Progress: A Revaluation," *Essays in Sociology and Social Philosophy* (New York, 1957–61), III, 5–6; Frankel, *The Case for Modern Man* (New York, 1956), 101–08. Peter Gay suggests that the *philosophes* had no "theory" of progress at all; better to think of them as tough-minded Stoics who occasionally dared to believe that man could improve his lot if he worked at it hard enough. Like Manuel, he apparently prefers to postpone the arrival of a thoroughgoing theory of progress until the early XIXth century. See Gay, *The Party of Humanity: Essays in the French Enlightenment* (New York, 1964), 270–73. Gay has also written a pungent critical reassessment of the Becker thesis, but he fails to discuss Becker's contention that the idea of progress was only a secularization of the Christian hope. Gay, "Carl Becker's Heavenly City," in Rockwood, *Carl Becker's Heavenly City Revisited*, 27–51, reprinted as ch. 7 in *The Party of Humanity*. Cf. Henry Vyverberg, *Historical Pessimism in the French Enlightenment* (Cambridge, Mass., 1958).

viving devotees are put on the defensive, which results perhaps in equally distorted judgments.

But certain caveats are worth uttering. The intellectual historian must be wary of seeing necessary casual links where none exists. Careful study of the actual historical flow of influence, wherever feasible, is always preferable to hypothesis and conjecture.[37] In particular, the intellectual historian should resist the temptation, with all the scholarly excitement about "symbol and myth," to leap to the conclusion that the borrowing of symbols from earlier periods necessarily also involves the borrowing of the ideational substance behind those symbols, or even proves a deep spiritual influence. He should not assume dogmatically that all ideas must evolve from other, older ideas, that spontaneous generation is impossible, or that non-intellectual factors cannot be decisive in originating new modes and currents of thought.

The intellectual historian must also be careful to avoid defining his concepts ahistorically. There is not one true, monolithic, gold-plated Idea of Progress, which emerges at a particular point in time, and against which all other so-called ideas of progress must be measured. Some of the difficulty in the historiographical debate over the origins of the idea of progress is certainly rooted in the too abstract and narrow definitions of that idea which scholars have demanded. There are, rather, many ideas of progress and where the lines are to be drawn and how the various types are to be discriminated historically is exceedingly difficult to determine. In tracing origins one might expect, for example, to find more direct links between Christianity and the ideas of progress in German thought from Kant to Hegel, than between Christianity and XVIIIth-century French ideas of progress.[38]

One further suggestion is, perhaps, not entirely out of order. Let us suppose that future scholars do find it impossible to document in convincing detail the influence of specifically Judeo-Christian ideas on the modern prophets of progress. A case may

[37] A formidable model for this sort of study is W. M. Simon's meticulous investigation of the influence of Comte, *European Positivism in the Nineteenth Century* (Ithaca, N.Y., 1963).

[38] Baillie's strategy of defining "layers" in the progressive tradition is a useful start in the right direction.

well be made, all over again, for the more or less independent origins of the progressive faith, and it may be argued that any civilization capable of producing a Galileo, a Descartes, a Newton, and a Locke would in due course have also brought forth an idea of progress, with or without the Judeo-Christian heritage. The fact will remain that only Western civilization produced a Galileo, a Descartes, a Newton, and a Locke. Underlying their thought, and the thought of Christianity, and the thought of the classical era, certain characteristically Western attitudes of mind may persist through all the vicissitudes of history in some form or other, and mark off the West from the civilizations of the Orient. To identify with some precision these *Urgestalten* [primitive forms] of Western thought might in time make a significant contribution to our understanding of how the Western mind in its modern phase of development arrived, under the appropriate historical stimuli, at ideas of progress. At least one may confidently predict that despite the self-assurance of the new orthodoxy, the question will remain open. The last words have not been spoken.

PART TWO

The Idea of Progress in Early Modern Times

1 Jean Bodin

Jean Bodin (1530-1596) was one of the most influential political thinkers of the Renaissance, best remembered today for his Six Books on the Republic, first published in 1576. Some years earlier, in 1565, he also wrote a treatise on history, with the expressed aim of discovering the principles of universal law through a more or less naturalistic inquiry into the whole history of mankind. In his seventh chapter, he attacks certain traditions in medieval historiography and, in particular, the myth of the "Golden Age." Bodin's defense of modern times does not perhaps constitute an idea of progress, but it helps prepare the way.

Once [according to erroneous interpretations of the Book of Daniel] there was a golden age, afterwards a silver, then a bronze, and then an iron. At length clay followed. But this opinion must be adjusted, for if anyone examines the meaning of historians, not of poets, certainly he will decide that there is a change in human affairs similar to that in the nature of all things; nor is there anything new under the sun, as that sage master of wisdom says.[1] The age which they call "golden," if it be compared with ours, would seem but iron. Who doubts that the flood came about through divine will on account of the sins of men, which were so many and so great that God himself was grieved that man had been created? Let us then consider the ages which followed the flood and are called "golden," not only by the poets, but also by Cato himself in his book *Of Origins*. He reported that Cameses and Saturn flourished at that time. But no one doubts that Cameses was called the son of Noah by the Hebrews; Saturn, Nimrod by

[1] Ecclesiastes 1:9.
SOURCE. Jean Bodin, *Method for the Easy Comprehension of History*, Beatrice Reynolds, translator, New York: Columbia University Press, 1945, pp. 296–302. Reprinted by permission of Columbia University Press. Copyright 1945 by Columbia University Press, New York.

the consent of all; it was his son Jupiter Belus who made an end to the golden age. From this it is plain that the golden age seemed a brief moment if an epoch of six thousand years is taken into account. Cato, following the fables of the poets, limited it to two hundred and fifty years. But how innocent was Cameses, who violated the honor of the best of parents by some new and disgraceful indignity! On this account he earned the curse of his father. It was even so in the case of Nimrod, grandson of Cameses, whom they call the founder of the golden age. What his character was is understood sufficiently from his very name, which in Hebrew means "rebel." He was termed by Moses a "mighty hunter," but he used this word everywhere to indicate robbers and wicked men, as even Aristotle placed piracy among the kinds of hunting. The next was Jupiter Belus, who with greater audacity, or shall I say impiety, hurled his aged father from power as if from a bridge. I observe there have been other Jupiters (for antiquity worshipped three hundred), but whichever is the one who drove his father from the throne, according to the poets, he is well known not only for parricide but also for all kinds of debauchery and incest with his sister. In that same era someone tried to snatch the tyranny from Jupiter. On this occasion the brothers[2] plotted to rend the skies, and when they had built towers and ramparts, they brought an accursed war against immortal God. They tried to cast him headlong from the sky [and would have succeeded], if they had not been prevented by a thunderbolt or by the confusion of tongues which made it impossible for the rebels to coöperate. On this account the name of Babylon was given to the tower which we call also Babel.

Of course Moses to a certain extent agreed with the poets (who confused the truth of the matter with fables). Yet what significance is there in the statement that the giants bring war against the gods—other than the struggle against nature, as Cicero says?

This, then, is that golden age which produced such monsters for us. I make the same judgment about Hercules who, Manetho reported, was the greatest of the pirates. He allied Theseus and

---

[2] In this sentence Bodin is combining two legends dealing with revolt against the Deity: the first is the revolt of the Titans, and the second, of the descendants of Noah who put up the tower of Babel in defiance of God.

Pirithous with him in criminal association, and when they had carried off Helen and had tried to take the daughter of King Molossus from her father, he threw them into prison. The one was torn by the Cerberean hounds; the other would have been torn in a short time, if he had not been called back from the infernal regions by the prayers of Hercules, or rather if he had not been saved for crueler punishments. Furthermore, who was stronger in all kinds of lust than Hercules, or shall I say more abominable? But lest these things should seem like fables, let us rather agree with Thucydides, the most truthful father of history. He left witness that a little before his time such was the barbarity and ferocity of men in Greece itself that by land and sea piracy was openly practiced. Without any shame travelers usually asked whether those they encountered were robbers or pirates or not. Yet since fortifications did not exist at that time and there were no defenses, justice resided in force, and the old colonists were continually driven from possession by new ones. This custom in Greece little by little became permanent. Moreover, the nations farthest removed from culture lived in this savagery for a long time, as Caesar wrote about the Germans. Piracy committed beyond the frontiers of each state is considered no disgrace among the Germans, and they recommend that this practice be used to train youth and to diminish laziness. From that custom, it happened, I suppose, that robbers, who are commonly called "brigands," take their name from the Brigantini, who hold Lake Podamicus or Brigantinus,[3] as the assassins do from that tribe of Persians which for a long time has labored under the bad reputation of being robbers and murderers. The Spartans, too, thought that there was no crime in the theft of edibles, but only in being caught stealing. Of course both opinions are more criminal than stealing, in so far as it is more wretched and base to permit freely by law anything which is wrong by nature.

These were the golden and the silver ages, in which men were scattered like beasts in the fields and the woods and had as much as they could keep by means of force and crime, until gradually they were reclaimed from that ferocity and barbarity to the re-

---

[3] Lake Constance.

finement of customs and the law-abiding society which we see about us. Thievery, which once incurred only a civil judgment, not only according to the laws of the Hebrews but also to those of the Greeks and the Latins, now everywhere in the world is repaid by capital punishment. On the contrary, if human affairs were becoming worse, long ago we should have reached the extreme limit of vices and improbity, whither indeed I think in times gone by they had arrived.

Since wicked men cannot progress any farther or stand any longer in the same place, it becomes necessary for them to retrace their steps gradually, forced either by shame, which inheres in men naturally, or by necessity, because society can in no way be developed by such crimes, or else they are forced by the goodness of God, which is the truer solution. This, indeed, becomes plain from books of annals and records of our elders, in which so many and dreadful enormities are reported (and yet not all) that we cannot very easily say which was the worst. The witnesses are Suetonius, Tacitus, Lampridius, and Athenaeus. What more criminal could be conceived than that the most horrible vices should be regarded as virtues? This is to be seen not only in depraved states but also in that republic which flourished under the institutions of Lycurgus and was thought most laudable by the consent of all writers. To omit the abandoned lusts of these people (Oh, that they were buried in eternal oblivion!), what is so impious as that men should be sacrificed most cruelly both at funerals and in religious rites? But this used to be done among almost all peoples. What more cruel than that the most innocent, under pretext of slavery, should be torn to bits in public spectacles, or should wound and kill each other for the delight of the people? Yet nothing was more commonplace among the Romans, who enjoyed the highest reputation for justice. By some divine retribution, in a spectacle of gladiators at Fidenae fifty thousand persons were overwhelmed in the collapse of one ampitheater. Certainly our men, much more wisely than the Romans (may it be said with due apologies to them), eliminated from the Christian state mortal contests among human beings, as well as the bloodthirsty spectacles of wild beasts, and set up instead a fruitful and useful kind of disputation on all subjects. How much better it is, then, to be formed for the good arts and true ornament than to be trained for the gymnasium? Yet we have not omitted suitable exercises for the body or neglected military training. Our records have also their Catos, Fabricii, Camilli, Alexanders, to say nothing of the others, and Titan did not fashion their hearts of a finer clay than our own.[4]

Was military glory greater in Alexander than in Charlemagne? The former, indeed, was great, but only against the soft Asiatics, as Caesar was wont to say about Pompey after he himself had experienced the strength of our men; the latter, our leader, conquered the most ferocious nations of Europe. Did an equal piety exist in Antoninus and in Louis the Pious? Moreover, what prince of all antiquity can be compared to St. Louis the king? Omitting the laws promulgated by him upon which this kingdom rests, certainly no such devotion of any prince toward God, responsibility to his country, love toward his subjects, and justice to all have ever been recorded. Not only the virtues of our men are equal to those of the ancients but also the disciplines. Literature suffers changes of fortune. First the arts arise in some places through the practice and the labor of talented men, then they develop, later they flourish for a while at a fixed level, then languish in their old age, and finally begin to die and are buried in a lasting oblivion by the eternal calamity of wars, or because too great abundance (an evil much to be feared in these times, of course) brings satiety to the frivolous, or because God inflicts just punishments upon those who direct useful knowledge to the ruin of men. Although disciplines had gradually developed among the Greeks, so that they believed these arts had reached their peak, such a change came about afterward that Greece herself, to judge from her present predicament, seems never to have existed.

What of the Latins? Among them talented men were so abundant that almost simultaneously they excelled all peoples in warlike glory and in superiority of culture. Yet by a similar fall they also started to lapse into their early barbarity when the forces of the Scythians, pouring into Italy, burned the well-stocked libraries almost everywhere and all the monuments of antiquity. This hor-

[4] Juvenal *Satire* xiv. 34.

rible deed destroyed all disciplines, so that for about a thousand years they lay prostrate without any prestige and indeed seemed to be dying, until Mansur, prince of Africa and Spain, stirred up the talents of the Arabs with offers of great rewards for the revival of letters. I omit how Egypt, India, and Ethiopia teemed with many philosophers, geometrists, and astrologers; how many well-known mathematicians were in Chaldea before Greece had any literature. I come back to our times in which, after a long eclipse of letters throughout almost the entire world, suddenly such a wealth of knowledge shone forth, such fertility of talents existed, as no age ever excelled.

Not even the Goths themselves have lacked the finest talents in modern times. Olaus Magnus is an evidence of this, as well as Holster and many others, as if nature had decreed that the wounds of knowledge should now be healed by those very people who once inflicted them. Although until recently they retained the custom of their ancestors and the voice of a herald ordered men of letters to depart from the senate (for we have evidence of this in their history), now everywhere they are wont to cultivate letters. This is so definite a change in all respects that no one ought to doubt that the same process occurs in human talent as in the fields, which are wont to repay with greater abundance the privilege of lying fallow. Some one will say, however, that the ancients were inventors of the arts and to them the glory ought to go. They certainly did discover many things—especially the power of the celestial bodies, the calculated courses of many stars—but yet not all—the wonderful trajections of fixed stars and of those called "planets." Then they noted carefully the obscurities of nature and explained many things accurately, and yet they left incomplete many of these things which have been completed and handed down to posterity by men of our time. No one, looking closely into this matter, can doubt that the discoveries of our men ought to be compared with the discoveries of our elders; many ought to be placed first. Although nothing is more remarkable in the whole nature of things than the magnet, yet the ancients were not aware of its use, clearly divine, and whereas they lived entirely within the Mediterranean basin, our men, on the other hand, traverse the whole earth every year in frequent voyages and lead colonies

into another world, as I might say, in order to open up the farthest recesses of India. Not only has this discovery developed an
abundant and profitable commerce (which formerly was insignificant or not well known) but also all men surprisingly work together in a world state, as if in one and the same city-state. Indeed,
in geography, one of the most excellent arts, one may understand
how much advance has been made from the fact that information
about India which used to seem fabulous to many (for Lactantius
and Augustine said that men who believed in the antipodes were
crazy) have been verified by us, as well as the motion of the fixed
stars and the trepidation of the great sphere. Moreover, what is
more remarkable than that abstraction and separation of forms
from matter (if I may speak thus)? From this the hidden secrets
of nature are revealed; hence healthful medicines are daily brought
forward. I pass over the method of investigating celestial longi-
tude from equal hours,[5] which could not be calculated by the
ancients from the normal to the ecliptic without great error. I
will not dwell upon the catapults of our ancestors and the ancient
engines of war, which, of course, seem like some boyish toy if
compared with our [instruments]. I omit finally countless arts,
both handicraft and weaving, with which the life of man has been
aided in a remarkable way. Printing alone can easily vie with all
the discoveries of all the ancients.

So they who say that all things were understood by the ancients
err not less than do those who deny them the early conquest of
many arts. Nature has countless treasures of knowledge which
cannot be exhausted in any age. Since these things are so and since
by some eternal law of nature the path of change seems to go in
a circle, so that vices press upon virtues, ignorance upon knowledge, base upon honorable, and darkness upon light, they are
mistaken who think that the race of men always deteriorates.
When old men err in this respect, it is understandable that this
should happen to them—that they sigh for the loss of the flower
of youth, which of itself breathes joy and cheerfulness. When
they see themselves deprived of every kind of delight and instead

---

[5] Hour in this sense was an angular measure of right ascension or longi-
tude, the 24th part of a great circle of the sphere, or 15 degrees.

of pleasure they feel sharp pains, instead of having unimpaired senses, they suffer weakness in all their members, it happens that they fall to these sad meditations and, deceived by the false picture of things, think that loyalty and friendship of man for man has died. As though returning from a distant journey, they narrate the golden century—the golden age—to the young men. But then their experience is the same as that of men carried out of port into the open sea—they think the houses and the town are departing from them; thus they think that delight, gentle conduct, and justice have flown to the heavens and deserted the earth.

2   *Bernard le Bovier de Fontenelle*

Like Bodin, Fontenelle (1657-1757) did not earn his place in intellectual history primarily as a student of philosophy of history, but he did contribute to the development of the idea of progress in the course of his career as a publicist for the achievements of modern science. Secretary of the Académie des Sciences from 1699 to 1741, he first attracted attention for his Conversations on the Plurality of Worlds, *published in 1686. This early work expounded, in layman's language, the universe according to Copernicus, Bruno, and Descartes. Two years later, he wrote a brief "Digression on the Ancients and the Moderns," which compared the philosophy, natural science, and literature of antiquity and modern times and, in so doing, put forward a theory of the necessary progress of knowledge. Fontenelle did not believe in moral or artistic progress but, in science and philosophy, he set no limits to human possibilities.*

Once thoroughly understood, the whole question of preeminence between the ancients and the moderns reduces itself to

SOURCE. Bernard le Bovier de Fontenelle, "Digression sur les Anciens et les Modernes," in *Oeuvres de Fontenelle*, Paris: Bastien, 1790, V, pp. 280–290 and 303–304. Translated for this book by W. Warren Wagar.

knowing if the trees formerly growing in our fields were larger than those of today. In the event that they were, Homer, Plato, and Demosthenes cannot be equalled in these latter days; but if our trees are as large as those of times past, we can equal Homer, Plato, and Demosthenes.

Let us explain this paradox. If the ancients had more intelligence than we, it must be that the brains of those times were better ordered, formed of firmer or more delicate fibers, filled with more animal spirits; but how could the brains of those times have been better ordered? The trees, then, would also have been larger and more beautiful; for if nature in that age was younger and more vigorous, the trees, as well as the brains of men, ought to have been able to feel this vigor and youth.

Let the admirers of the ancients take a little care, when they tell us that those people are the sources of good taste and reason, and the lights destined to illuminate all other men, that one is intelligent only insofar as he admires them, that nature exhausted herself in producing those great originals. In truth they make them out to belong to a different species from our own, but physics does not agree with all these pretty phrases. Nature has in hand a certain paste which is always the same, which she turns this way and that, unceasingly, in a thousand different ways, and from which she forms men, animals, and plants; and certainly she has not formed Plato, Demosthenes, or Homer from a clay finer or better prepared than our philosophers, orators, and poets of today. I am concerned here only with the relationship between our minds, which are not material in nature, and our brains, which are material, and which by their various arrangements produce all the differences existing between minds.

But if the trees of all the centuries are equally large, the trees of all the countries are not. There are differences also in minds. Different ideas are like plants or flowers which do not flourish equally well in all kinds of climates. Perhaps our French soil is not suited to the type of reasoning done by the Egyptians, any more than to their palm trees; and without going so far, perhaps the orange trees, which do not flourish here as easily as they do in Italy, indicate that in Italy they have a certain turn of mind which is not quite the same as ours in France. It is in all respects certain that as a result of the connection and interdependence which exists among all the parts of the material world, the differences of climate which are felt by plants must extend to brains, and have some effect upon them.

Nevertheless, this latter effect is not so strong or obvious because art and culture can do much more with brains than with soil, which is composed of matter more hard and intractable. Thus, a country's thoughts are more easily transferred to another country than its plants, and we would not have so much trouble importing the Italian genius into our work as we would raising orange trees.

It seems to me that in most people's judgment there is more diversity among minds than among faces. I am not quite sure of this. Faces, by simply looking at one another, take on no new resemblances; but minds do take them on, as a result of their intercourse one with another. Thus minds, which in the natural course of things would differ as much as faces, come to differ rather less.

The facility that minds have in modelling themselves upon others has the effect that peoples do not preserve the original intellects which they derived from their climates. The reading of Greek books produces in us the same effect as if we married only Greeks. It is certain that through alliances so frequent the blood of Greece and that of France would be altered, and that the facial appearance peculiar to each nation would change somewhat.

Besides, since one cannot judge which climates are the most favorable for the mind, since they apparently have advantages and disadvantages which counterbalance one another, and since those which might give rise to more liveliness might also give rise to less preciseness, and so forth, it follows that differences of climate may be held of no account, provided that the minds are otherwise equally cultured. The most one could assume is that the torrid and the two glacial zones are not suitable for the sciences. Down to the present, they have not developed beyond Egypt and Mauritania on one side and Sweden on the other; perhaps it has not been by chance that they have been restricted to the area bounded by Mt. Atlas and the Baltic Sea: we cannot be sure that these are not the boundaries which nature has drawn for them, or that great Lappish or Negro scientists are ever to be expected.

However this may be, here, it seems to me, lies the answer to the great question of the ancients and the moderns. The centuries create no natural distinctions among men. The climates of Greece or of Italy, and the climate of Frances, are too similar to lead to any perceptible difference between the Greeks or the Latins and ourselves. Even if they should produce such a difference, it would be quite easy to efface, and in the end it would be no more to their advantage than to ours. We are all then perfectly equal, ancients and moderns, Greeks, Latins, and Frenchmen.

I do not maintain that this argument will appear persuasive to everyone. If I had made use of great turns of eloquence, if I had set in juxtaposition historical evidence which does honor to the moderns with other historical evidence which does honor to the ancients, and passages favorable to the one party with passages favorable to the other; if I had called those scholars fatuous who call us ignorant and shallow, and, according to the conventions which govern the behavior of literary folk, if I had paid out injury for injury with exactitude to the partisans of antiquity, perhaps my arguments would have been better received: but it appeared to me that to manage the affair in this manner would be never to make an end of it, and that after many beautiful declamations on one side and the other, we should be astonished to learn that we had got nowhere. I decided that the shorter way was to consult physics a little on all this, a science which possesses the secret of severely abridging the disputes which rhetoric renders endless.

Here, for example, after we have acknowledged the natural equality which exists between the ancients and ourselves, there remains no further difficulty. We see clearly that all differences, whatever they may be, must be caused by extraneous circumstances, such as weather, government, or the general state of affairs.

The ancients invented everything: it is with this point that their partisans triumph; hence the ancients had much greater minds than ours. But not at all; they merely lived before us. I would as soon like to see them praised for having been the first to drink water from our rivers, and ourselves abused for drinking only what they left behind. If we had been in their place, we would have done the inventing; if they were in ours, they would be adding to what they found invented: there is no great mystery here.

I do not speak now of the inventions which chance brings into existence, and through which it can give honor, if it pleases, to the most unskillful man on earth; I am speaking only of those inventions which have demanded some thought and some mental effort. It is certain that the humblest of these have been reserved for men of extraordinary genius, and that in the infancy of the world all that Archimedes could have done would have been to invent the plow. Placed in another century, Archimedes burned the ships of the Romans with mirrors, if, however, this is not just a fable.

He who wanted to make specious and brilliant points would maintain, to the glory of the moderns, that the mind needs no great effort for the first discoveries, and that nature seems to bring us to them herself, but that more effort is needed to add something to them, and still greater effort the more has been added already, because the matter at hand is more fully exploited, and that which remains to be discovered is less exposed to view. Perhaps the admirers of the ancients would not neglect an argument as good as this, if it favored their side, but I must in good faith confess that it is not really as sound as all that.

It is true that to add to the first discoveries, more mental effort is often needed than was required to make them in the first place; but then we also find such an effort far easier to make. By these same discoveries that we have before our eyes, our minds have already been enlightened; our own vision is supplemented by what we borrow from others; and if we surpass the first inventor, it is he himself who has helped us surpass him. Therefore he always has his share of the glory of our work, and were he to take back what belongs to him, no more would be left for us than for him.

I carry justice so far in this regard that I even give credit to the ancients for the infinite number of false opinions they had, the bad reasoning they did, the foolish things they uttered. Our condition is such that we cannot arrive at reasonable positions all at once on any matter whatever; before that we must go astray for a great while, and pass through various sorts of errors and stages of silliness. It should always have been quite simple, so it seems, to take it into our heads that the whole play of nature consists of forms and the movements of bodies: but before coming to that point, it was necessary to try out the Ideas of Plato, the Numbers of Pythagoras, the Qualities of Aristotle; and when all that was seen to be false, we were reduced to adopting the true system. I say that we were reduced to it, for in truth there remained no other, and it does seem that we forbade ourselves from adopting it for as long a time as we possibly could. We are in the debt of the ancients for having exhausted the greater part of the false ideas that could be conceived; it was absolutely necessary to pay to error and ignorance the tribute which they paid, and we must not lack gratitude toward those who have acquitted us of this responsibility. It is the same with various matters, concerning which we should have uttered I know not how many foolish things if they had not already been uttered, and if, so to speak, we had not been relieved of them; even so, there are sometimes moderns who take them up again, perhaps because they have not yet been said as often as necessary, Thus, enlightened by the views of the ancients, and even by their faults, we not surprisingly surpass them. Only to equal them would require that our nature be very much inferior to theirs; it would almost require that we not be as human as they were.

Nevertheless, in order that the moderns may always outstrip the ancients, conditions must be of the sort that permits this to happen. Eloquence and poetry demand only a certain number of views, limited in relation to other arts, and they depend principally on the liveliness of the imagination. Now in a few centuries men can have accumulated a small number of these views; and liveliness of imagination has no need of a long succession of experiences, or a great quantity of rules, to attain all the perfection of which it is capable. But physics, medicine, and mathematics are composed of an infinite number of views, and depend on exact reasoning, which perfects itself with extreme slowness, and is always in process of perfecting itself. It is often even necessary that they be aided by the experiences to which chance alone can give birth, and which it does not bring about at some appointed time. Clearly all this has no end, and the latest physicists or mathematicians ought naturally to be the most skilled.

And, in fact, what is basic in philosophy, and extends from there to everything else, I mean the method of reasoning, has been vastly perfected in this century. I very much doubt that the majority of people will agree with the remark that I am about to make: I shall make it nonetheless, for those who are skilled in reasoning; and I may pride myself that it takes courage to expose onself in the interests of truth to the criticism of all those others, whose number is surely far from contemptible. Whatever the subject may be, the ancients are rather inclined not to reason perfectly. Often feeble consonances, petty likenesses, unsubstantial witticisms, vague and confused arguments pass with them for proofs; it costs them nothing to prove a point; but what an ancient demonstrates with ease would nowadays give much trouble to a poor modern; for what rigor do we not insist upon in our reasonings? We demand that they be intelligible, we demand that they be exact, we demand that they come to conclusions. We malignantly point out the slighest equivocation, whether of ideas or of words; we harshly condemn the most ingenious thing in the world, if it does not get down to the facts. Before Descartes, people reasoned more comfortably; past centuries were very lucky not to have had that man. It is he, in my judgment, who has brought about this new method of reasoning, much more praiseworthy even than his philosophic system, of which a good part has been found false or very uncertain, according to the very rules that he taught us. In short, there reigns a precision and an exactness hitherto scarcely known, not only in our good works of physics and metaphysics, but also in those of religion, morals, and criticism.

I am even strongly persuaded that these works will be carried still further. Into our best books the reasonings of antiquity still slip: but one day we shall be ancients; and will it not be just that our posterity, in its turn, should correct and surpass us, principally in the method of reasoning, which is a science in itself, and the most difficult, and the least cultivated of all?

*   *   *

If the great men of this century had charitable sentiments toward posterity, they would caution it not to admire them too much, and to aspire always at least to equal them. Nothing so much arrests the progress of things, nothing so much limits minds as excessive admiration for the ancients. Because men were devoted to the authority of Aristotle and searched for truth only in his enigmatic writings, and never in nature, not only did philosophy make no progress, but it fell into an abyss of balderdash and unintelligible ideas, from which it has taken all the trouble in the world to retrieve it. Aristotle never produced a true philosopher, but he has throttled a good many who might have become philosophers, if the opportunity had arisen. And the bad thing is that once a fantasy of this sort has been established among men, it lasts a long time; it takes whole centuries to get away from it, even after its absurdity has been recognized. If men one day became infatuated with Descartes, and put him in Aristotle's place, it would be very nearly as objectionable.

But we must examine all possibilities: it is not certain that posterity will count to our credit the two or three thousand years that one day will separate us from it, as we count them to the credit of the Greeks and Latins today. It seems quite likely that reason will be perfected, and that men will generally cast off crude prejudice in favor of antiquity. Perhaps it will not last much longer; perhaps nowadays we admire the ancients in vain, and without prospect of ever being admired in the same way ourselves. That would be rather a pity!

PART THREE
Classical Formulations

1 Immanuel Kant

Scientist, epistemologist, metaphysician, aesthetician, moralist, Immanuel Kant (1724-1804) "is generally considered the greatest of modern philosophers," as Bertrand Russell reports in his History of Western Philosophy. *Whole courses are devoted to Kant at both the undergraduate and the graduate level, and hundreds of philosophers have spent the better part of their lives studying his thought. The attention paid in commentaries on the idea of progress to its many French protagonists sometimes leads us to overlook the importance of Kant's great essay on universal history published in 1784, which is reprinted below in its entirety. Here Kant distills much of the best thought of the European Enlightenment on the meaning of history and provides a classical formulation of the idea of general progress. Like many later prophets of progress, Kant believes that mankind is destined to achieve universal peace through the establishment of some form of world government.*

Whatever metaphysical theory may be formed regarding the freedom of the will, it holds equally true that the manifestations of the will in human actions, are determined like all other external events, by universal natural laws. Now history is occupied with the narration of these manifestations as facts, however deeply their causes may lie concealed. Hence in view of this natural principle of regulation, it may be hoped that when the play of the freedom of the human will is examined on the great scale of universal history, a regular march will be discovered in its movements; and that, in this way, what appears to be tangled and unregulated in the case of individuals, will be recognised in the

SOURCE. Immanuel Kant, "Idea of a Universal History from a Cosmopolitical Point of View," in William Hastie, editor and translator, *Principles of Politics*, Edinburgh: T. & T. Clark, 1891, pp. 1–29. Reprinted by permission of T. & T. Clark.

history of the whole species as a continually advancing, though slow, development of its original capacities and endowments. Thus marriages, births and deaths appear to be incapable of being reduced to any rule by which their numbers might be calculated beforehand, on account of the great influence which the free will of man exercises upon them; and yet the annual statistics of great countries prove that these events take place according to constant natural laws. In this respect they may be compared with the very inconstant changes of the weather which cannot be determined beforehand in detail, but which yet, on the whole, do not fail to maintain the growth of plants, the flow of rivers, and other natural processes, in a uniform uninterrupted course. Individual men, and even whole nations, little think, while they are pursuing their own purposes—each in his own way and often one in direct opposition to another—that they are advancing unconsciously under the guidance of a purpose of nature which is unknown to them, and that they are toiling for the realisation of an end which, even if it were known to them, might be regarded as of little importance.

Men, viewed as a whole, are not guided in their efforts merely by instinct, like the lower animals; nor do they proceed in their actions, like the citizens of a purely rational world, according to a preconcerted plan. And so it appears as if no regular systematic history of mankind would be possible, as in the case, for instance, of bees and beavers. Nor can one help feeling a certain repugnance in looking at the conduct of men as it is exhibited on the great stage of the world. With glimpses of wisdom appearing in individuals here and there, it seems, on examining it externally as if the whole web of human history were woven out of folly and childish vanity and the frenzy of destruction, so that at the end one hardly knows what idea to form of our race, albeit so proud of its prerogatives. In such circumstances, there is no resource for the philosopher but, while recognizing the fact that a rational conscious purpose cannot be supposed to determine mankind in the play of their actions as a whole, to try whether he cannot discover a universal purpose of nature in this paradoxical movement of human things, and whether in view of this purpose, a history of creatures who proceed without a plan of their own, may nevertheless be possible according to a determinate plan of nature. We will accordingly see whether we can succeed in finding a clue to such a history; and in the event of doing so, we shall then leave it to nature to bring forth the man who will be fit to compose it. Thus did she bring forth a Kepler who, in an unexpected way, reduced the eccentric paths of the planets to definite laws; and then she brought forth a Newton, who explained those laws by a universal natural cause.

First Proposition: All the capacities implanted in a creature by nature, are destined to unfold themselves, completely and conformably to their end, in the course of time.

This proposition is established by observation, external as well as internal or anatomical, in the case of all animals. An organ which is not to be used, or an arrangement which does not attain its end, is a contradiction in the teleological science of nature. For, if we turn away from that fundamental principle, we have then before us a nature moving without a purpose, and no longer conformable to law; and the cheerless gloom of chance takes the place of the guiding light of reason.

Second Proposition: In man, as the only rational creature on earth, those natural capacities which are directed towards the use of his reason, could be completely developed only in the species and not in the individual.

Reason, in a creature, is a faculty of which it is characteristic to extend the laws and purposes involved in the use of all its powers far beyond the sphere of natural instinct, and it knows no limit in its efforts. Reason, however, does not itself work by instinct, but requires experiments, exercise and instruction in order to advance gradually from one stage of insight to another. Hence each individual man would necessarily have to live an enormous length of time in order to learn by himself how to make a complete use of all his natural endowments. Otherwise, if nature should have given him but a short lease of life—as is actually the case—reason would then require the production of an almost inconceivable series of generations, the one handing down its enlightenment to the other, in order that her germs, as implanted in our species may be at last unfolded to that stage of development which is completely conformable to her inherent design. And the point of time at which this is to be reached, must, at least in idea, form the goal and aim of man's endeavours, because his natural capacities would otherwise have to be regarded as, for the most part, purposeless and bestowed in vain. But such a view would abolish all our practical principles, and thereby also throw on nature the suspicion of practising a childish play in the case of man alone, while her wisdom must otherwise be recognized as a fundamental principle in judging of all other arrangements.

Third Proposition: Nature has willed that man shall produce wholly out of himself all that goes beyond the mechanical structure and arrangement of his animal existence, and that he shall participate in no other happiness or perfection but what he has procured for himself, apart from instinct, by his own reason.

Nature, according to this view, does nothing that is superfluous and is not prodigal in the use of means for her ends. As she gave man reason and freedom of will on the basis of reason, this was at once a clear indication of her purpose in respect of his endowments. With such equipment, he was not to be guided by instinct, nor furnished and instructed by innate knowledge; much rather must he produce everything out of himself. The invention of his own covering and shelter from the elements, and the means of providing for his external security and defence,—for which nature gave him neither the horns of the bull, nor the claws of the lion, nor the fangs of the dog,—as well as all the sources of delight which could make life agreeable, his very insight and prudence, and even the goodness of his will, all these were to be entirely his own work. Nature seems to have taken pleasure in exercising her utmost parsimony in this case and to have measured her animal equipments very sparingly. She seems to have exactly fitted them to the most necessitous requirements of the mere beginning of an existence, as if it had been her will that man, when he had at last struggled up from the greatest crudeness of life to the highest capability and to internal perfection in his habit of thought, and thereby also—so far as it is possible on earth— to happiness, should claim the merit of it as all his own and owe it only to himself. It thus looks as if nature had laid more upon his rational self-esteem than upon his mere well-being. For in this movement of human life, a great host of toils and troubles wait upon man. It appears, however, that the purpose of nature was not so much that he should have an agreeable life, but that he should carry forward his own self-culture until he made himself worthy of life and well-being. In this connection it is always a subject of wonder that the older generations appear only to pursue their weary toil for the sake of those who come after them, preparing for the latter another stage on which they may carry higher the structure which nature has in view; and that it is to be the happy fate of only the latest generations to dwell in the building upon which the long series of their forefathers have laboured, without so much as intending it and yet with no possibility of participating in the happiness which they are preparing. Yet, however mysterious this may be, it is as necessary as it is mysterious, when we once accept the position that one species of animals was destined to possess reason, and that, forming a class of rational beings mortal in all the individuals but immortal in the species, it was yet to attain to a complete development of its capacities.

Fourth Proposition: The means which nature employs to bring about the development of all the capacities implanted in men, is their mutual antagonism in society, but only so far as this antagonism becomes at length the cause of an order among them that is regulated by law.

By this antagonism, I mean the unsocial sociability of men; that is, their tendency to enter into society, conjoined, however, with an accompanying resistance which continually threatens to dissolve this society. The disposition for this lies manifestly in human nature. Man has an inclination to socialise himself by associating with others, because in such a state he feels himself more than a natural man, in the development of his natural capacities. He has, moreover, a great tendency to individualise himself by isolation from others, because he likewise finds in himself the unsocial disposition of wishing to direct everything merely according to his own mind; and hence he expects resistance everywhere just as he knows with regard to himself that he is inclined on his part to resist others. Now it is this resistance or mutual antagonism that awakens all the powers of man, that drives him to overcome all his propensity to indolence, and that impels him, through the desire of honour or power of wealth, to strive after rank among his fellow-men—whom he can neither bear to interfere with himself, nor yet let alone. Then the first real steps are taken from the rudeness of barbarism to the culture of civilisation, which particularly lies in the social worth of man. All his talents are now gradually developed, and with the progress of enlightenment a beginning is made in the institution of a mode of thinking which can transform the crude natural capacity for moral distinctions, in the course of time, into definite practical principles of action; and thus a pathologically constrained combination into a form of society, is developed at last to a moral and rational whole. Without those qualities of an unsocial kind, out of which this antagonism arises—which viewed by themselves are certainly not amiable but which everyone must necessarily find in the movements of his own selfish propensities—men might have led an Arcadian shepherd life in complete harmony, contentment and mutual love, but in that case all their talents would have forever remained hidden in their germ. As gentle as the sheep they tended, such men would hardly have won for their existence a higher worth than belonged to their domesticated cattle; they would not have filled up with their rational nature the void remaining in the creation, in respect of its final end. Thanks be then to nature for this unsociableness, for this envious jealousy and vanity, for this unsatiable desire of possession, or even of power! Without them all the excellent capacities implanted in mankind by nature, would slumber eternally undeveloped. Man wishes concord; but nature knows better what is good for his species, and she will have discord. He wishes to live comfortably and pleasantly; but nature wills that, turning from idleness and inactive contentment, he shall throw himself into toil and suffering even in order to find out remedies against them, and to extricate his life prudently from them again. The natural impulses that urge man in this direction, the sources of that unsociableness and general antagonism from which so many evils arise, do yet at the same time impel him to new exertion of his powers, and consequently, to further development of his natural capacities. Hence, they clearly manifest the arrangement of a wise Creator, and do not at all, as is often supposed, betray the hand of a malevolent spirit that has deteriorated His glorious creation, or spoiled it from envy.

Fifth Proposition: The greatest practical problem for the human race, to the solution of which it is compelled by nature, is the establishment of a civil society, universally administering right according to law.

It is only in a society which possesses the greatest liberty, and which consequently involves a thorough antagonism of its members—with, however, the most exact determination and guarantee of the limits of this liberty in order that it may coexist with the liberty of others—that the highest purpose of nature, which is the development of all her capacities, can be attained in the case of mankind. Now nature also wills that the human race shall attain through itself to this, as to all the other ends for which it was destined. Hence a society in which liberty under external laws may be found combined in the greatest possible degree with irresistible power, or a perfectly just civil constitution, is the highest natural problem prescribed to the human species. And this is so, because nature can only by means of the solution and fulfillment of this problem, realise her other purposes with our race. A certain necessity compels man, who is otherwise so greatly prepossessed in favour of unlimited freedom, to enter into this state of coercion and restraint. And indeed, it is the greatest necessity of all that does this; for it is created by men themselves whose inclinations make it impossible for them to exist long beside each other in wild lawless freedom. But in such a complete growth as the civil union, these very inclinations afterwards produce the best effects. It is with them as with the trees in a forest; for just because everyone strives to deprive the other of air and sun, they compel each other to seek them both above, and thus they grow beautiful and straight, whereas those that in freedom and apart from one another shoot out their branches at will, grow stunted and crooked and awry. All the culture and art that adorn humanity, and the fairest social order, are fruits of that unsociableness which is necessitated of itself to discipline itself and which thus constrains man, by compulsive art, to develop completely the germs of his nature.

Sixth Proposition: This problem is likewise the most difficult of its kind, and it is the latest to be solved by the human race.

The difficulty which the mere idea of this problem brings into view, is that man is an animal, and if he lives among others of his kind he has need of a master. For he certainly misuses his freedom in relation to his fellow-men; and, although as a rational creature, he desires a law which may set bounds to the freedom of all, yet his own selfish animal inclinations lead him wherever he can, to except himself from it. He, therefore, requires a master to break his self-will, and compel him to obey a will that is universally valid, and in relation to which everyone may be free. Where, then, does he obtain this master? Nowhere but in the human race. But this master is an animal too, and also requires a master. Begin, then, as he may, it is not easy to see how he can procure a supreme authority over public justice that would be essentially just, whether such an authority may be sought in a single person or in a society of many selected persons. The highest authority has to be just in itself, and yet to be a man. This problem is, therefore, the most difficult of its kind; and, indeed, its perfect solution is impossible. Out of such crooked material as man is made of, nothing can be hammered quite straight. So it is only an approximation to this idea that is imposed upon us by nature. It further follows that this problem is the last to be practically worked out, because it requires correct conceptions of the nature of a possible constitution, great experience founded on the practice of ages, and above all a good will prepared for the reception of the solution. But these three conditions could not easily be found together; and if they are found it can only be very late in time, and after many attempts to solve the problem had been made in vain.

Seventh Proposition: The problem of the establishment of a perfect civil constitution is dependent on the problem of the regulation of the external relations between the states conformably to law; and without the solution of this latter problem it cannot be solved.

What avails it to labour at the arrangement of a commonwealth as a civil constitution regulated by law among individual men? The same unsociableness which forced men to it, becomes again the cause of each commonwealth assuming the attitude of uncontrolled freedom in its external relations, that is, as one state in relation to other states; and consequently, any one state must expect from any other the same sort of evils as oppressed individual men and compelled them to enter into a civil union regulated by law. Nature has accordingly again used the unsociableness of men, and even of great societies and political bodies, her creatures of this kind, as a means to work out through their mutual antagonism a condition of rest and security. She works through wars, through the strain of never relaxed preparation for them, and through the necessity which every state is at last compelled to feel within itself, even in the midst of peace, to begin some imperfect efforts to carry out her purpose. And, at last, after many devastations, overthrows, and even complete internal exhaustion of their powers, the nations are driven forward to the goal which reason might have well impressed upon them, even without so much sad experience. This is none other than the advance out of the lawless state of savages and the entering into a Federation of Nations. It is thus brought about that every state, including even the smallest, may rely for its safety and its rights, not on its own power or its own judgment of right, but only on this great international federation (*Foedus Amphictionum*), on its combined power, and on the decision of the common will according to laws. However visionary this idea may appear to be—and it has been ridiculed in the way in which it has been presented by an Abbé de St. Pierre or Rousseau (perhaps because they believed its realisation to be so near)—it is nevertheless the inevitable issue of the necessity in which men involve one another. For this necessity must compel the nations to be the very resolution—however hard it may appear —to which the savage in his uncivilized state, was so unwillingly compelled, when he had to surrender his brutal liberty and seek rest and security in a constitution regulated by law. All wars are, accordingly, so many attempts—not, indeed, in the intention of men, but yet according to the purpose of nature—to bring about new relations between the nations; and by destruction or at least dismemberment of them all, to form new political corporations. These new organisations, again, are not capable of being preserved either in themselves or beside one another, and they must therefore pass in turn through similar new revolutions, till at last, partly by the best possible arrangement of the civil constitution within, and partly by common convention and legislation without, a condition will be attained, which, in the likeness of a civil commonwealth and after the manner of an automaton, will be able to preserve itself.

Three views may be put forward as to the way in which this condition is to be attained. In the first place, it may be held that from an Epicurean concourse of causes in action, it is to be expected that the states, like the little particles of matter, will try by their fortuitous conjunctions all sort of formations which will be again destroyed by new collisions, till at last some one constitution will by *chance* succeed in preserving itself in its proper form, —a lucky accident which will hardly ever come about! In the second place, it may rather be maintained that nature here pursues a regular march in carrying our species up from the lower stage of animality to the highest stage of humanity, and that this is done by a compulsive art that is inherent in man, whereby his natural capacities and endowments are developed in perfect regularity through an apparently wild disorder. Or, in the third place, it may even be asserted, that out of all these actions and reactions of men as a whole, nothing at all—or at least nothing rational— will ever be produced; that it will be in the future as it has ever been in the past, and that no one will ever be able to say whether the discord which is so natural to our species, may not be preparing for us, even in this civilised state of society, a hell of evils at the end; nay, that it is not perhaps advancing even now to annihilate again by barbaric devastation, this actual state of society and all progress hitherto made in civilisation,—a fate against which there is no guarantee under a government of blind chance, identical as it is with lawless freedom in action, unless a connecting wisdom is covertly assumed to underlie the system of nature. Now, which of these views is to be adopted, depends almost entirely on the question, whether it is rational to recognise harmony and design in the parts of the constitution of nature and to deny them of the whole? We have glanced at what has been done by the seemingly purposeless state of savages; how it checked for a time all the natural capacities of our species but at last by the very evils in which it involved mankind, it compelled them to pass from this state, and to enter into a civil constitution, in which all the germs of humanity could be unfolded. And, in like manner, the barbarian freedom of the states when once they were founded, proceeded in the same way of progress. By the expenditure of all the resources of the commonwealth in military preparations against each other, by the devastations occasioned by war, and still more by the necessity of holding themselves continually in readiness for it, the full development of the capacities of mankind are undoubtedly retarded in their progress; but, on the other hand, the very evils which thus arise, compel men to find out means against them. A law of equilibrium is thus discovered for the regulation of the really wholesome antagonism of contiguous states as it springs up out of their freedom; and a united power, giving emphasis to this law, is constituted, whereby there is introduced a universal condition of public security among the nations. And that the powers of mankind may not fall asleep, this condition is not entirely free from danger; but it is at the same time not without a principle which operates, so as to equalise the mutual action and reaction of the powers, that they may not destroy each other. Before the last step of bringing in a universal union of the states is taken—and accordingly when human nature is only half way in its progress—it has to endure the hardest evils of all, under the deceptive semblance of outward prosperity; and Rousseau was not so far wrong when he preferred the state of the savages, if the last stage which our race has yet to surmount be left out of view. We are cultivated in a high degree by science and art. We are civilized, even to excess, in the way of all sorts of social forms of politeness and elegance. But there is still much to be done before we can be regarded as moralised. The idea of morality certainly belongs to real culture; but an application of this idea which extends no farther than the likeness of morality in the sense of honour and external propriety, merely constitutes civilisation. So long, however, as states lavish all their resources upon vain and violent schemes of aggrandisement, so long as they continually impede the slow movements of the endeavour to cultivate the newer habits of thought and character on the part of the citizens, and even withdraw from them all the means of furthering it, nothing in the way of moral progress can be expected. A long internal process of improvement is thus required in every commonwealth as a condition for the higher culture of its citizens. But all apparent good that is not grafted upon a morally good disposition, is nothing but mere illusion and glittering misery. In this condition the human race will remain until it shall have worked istelf, in the way that has been indicated, out of the existing chaos of its political relations.

Eighth Proposition: The history of the human race, viewed as a whole, may be regarded as the realisation of a hidden plan of nature to bring about a political constitution, internally, and, for this purpose, also externally perfect, as the only state in which all the capacities implanted by her in mankind can be fully developed.

This proposition is a corollary from the preceding proposition. We see by it that philosophy may also have its millenial view, but in this case, the chiliasm is of such a nature that the very idea of it—although only in a far-off way—may help to further its realisation; and such a prospect is, therefore, anything but visionary. The real question is, whether experience discloses anything of such a movement in the purpose of nature. I can only say it does a little; for the movement in this orbit appears to require such a long time till it goes full round, that the form of its path and the relation of its parts to the whole, can hardly be determined out of the small portion which the human race has yet passed through in this relation. The determination of this problem is just as difficult and uncertain as it is to calculate from all previous astronomical observations what course our sun, with the whole host of his attendant train, is pursuing in the great system of the fixed stars, although on the ground of the total arrangement of the structure of the universe and the little that has been observed of it, we may infer, confidently enough, to the result of such a movement. Human nature, however, is so constituted that it cannot be indifferent even in regard to the most distant epoch that may affect our race, if only it can be expected with certainty. And such indifference is the less possible in the case before us when it appears that we might by our own rational arrangements hasten the coming of this joyous period for our descendants. Hence the faintest traces of the approach of this period will be very important to ourselves. Now the states are already involved in the present day in such close relations with each other, that none of them can pause or slacken in its internal civilisation without losing power and influence in relation to the rest; and, hence the maintenance, if not the progress, of this end of nature is, in a manner, secured even by the ambitious designs of the states themselves. Further, civil liberty cannot now be easily assailed without inflicting such damage as will be felt in all trades and industries, and especially in commerce; and this would entail a diminution of the powers of the state in external relations. This liberty, moreover, gradually advances further. But if the citizen is hindered in seeking his prosperity in any way suitable to himself that is consistent with the liberty of others the activity of business is checked generally; and thereby the powers of the whole state, again, are weakened. Hence the restrictions on personal liberty of action are always more and more removed, and universal liberty even in religion comes to be conceded. And thus it is that, notwithstanding the intrusion of many a delusion and caprice, the spirit of enlightenment gradually arises as a great good which the human race must derive even from the selfish purposes of aggrandisement on the part of its rulers, if they understand what is for their own advantage. This enlightenment, however, and along with it a certain sympathetic interest which the enlightened man cannot avoid taking in the good which he perfectly understands, must by and by pass up to the throne and exert an influence even upon the principles of government. Thus although our rulers at present have no money to spend on public educational institutions, or in general on all that concerns the highest good of the world—because all their resources are already placed to the account of the next war—yet they will certainly find it to be to their own advantage at least not to hinder the people in their own efforts in this direction, however weak and slow these may be. Finally, war itself comes to be regarded as a very hazardous and objectionable undertaking, not only from its being so artificial in itself and so uncertain as regards its issue on both sides, but also from the after pains which the state feels in the ever-increasing burdens it entails in the form of national debt—a modern infliction —which it becomes almost impossible to extinguish. And to this is to be added the influence which every political disturbance of any state of our continent—linked as it is so closely to others by the connections of trade—exerts upon all the states and which becomes so observable that they are forced by their common danger, although without lawful authority, to offer themselves as arbiters in the troubles of any such state. In doing so, they are beginning to arrange for a great future political body, such as the world has never yet seen. Although this political body may as yet exist only in a rough outline, nevertheless a feeling begins, as it were, to stir in all its members, each of which has a common interest in the maintenance of the whole. And this may well inspire the hope that after many political revolutions and transformations, the highest purpose of nature will be at last realised in the establishment of a universal cosmopolitical institution, in the bosom of which all the original capacities and endowments of the human species will be unfolded and developed.

Ninth Proposition: A philosophical attempt to work out the universal history of the world according to the plan of nature in its aiming at a perfect civil union, must be regarded as possible, and as even capable of helping forward the purpose of nature.

It seems, at first sight, a strange and even an absurd proposal to suggest the composition of a history according to the idea of how the course of the world must proceed, if it is to be conformable to certain rational laws. It may well appear that only a romance could be produced from such a point of view. However, if it be assumed that nature, even in the play of human freedom, does not proceed without plan and design, the idea may well be regarded as practicable; and, although we are too short sighted to see through the secret mechanism of her constitution, yet the idea may be serviceable as a clue to enable us to penetrate the otherwise planless aggregate of human actions as a whole, and to represent them as constituting a system. For the idea may so far

be easily verified. Thus, suppose we start from the history of
Greece, as that by which all the older contemporaneous history
has been preserved, or at least accredited to us. Then, if we study
its influence upon the formation and malformation of the political
institutions of the Roman people, which swallowed up the Greek
states, and if we further follow the influence of the Roman Empire upon the barbarians who destroyed it in turn, and continue
this investigation down to our own day, conjoining with it epi-
sodically the political history of other peoples according as the
knowledge of them has gradually reached us through these more
enlightened nations, we shall discover a regular movement of
progress through the political institutions of our continent, which
is probably destined to give laws to all other parts of the world.
Applying the same method of study everywhere, both to the
internal civil constitutions and laws of the states, and to their
external relations to each other, we see how in both relations the
good they contained served for a certain period to elevate and
glorify particular nations, and with themselves, their arts and
sciences,—until the defects attaching to their institutions came in
time to cause their overthrow. And yet their very ruin leaves
always a germ of growing enlightenment behind, which being
further developed by every revolution, acts as a preparation for a
subsequent higher stage of progress and improvement. Thus, as
I believe, we can discover a clue which may serve for more than
the explanation of the confused play of human things, or for the
art of political prophecy in reference to future changes in states,
—a use which has been already made of the history of mankind,
even although it was regarded as the incoherent effect of an unregulated freedom! Much more than all this is attained by the
idea of human history viewed as founded upon the assumption of
a universal plan in nature. For this idea gives us a new ground
of hope, as it opens up to us a consoling view of the future, in
which the human species is represented in the far distance as
having at last worked itself up to a condition in which all the
germs implanted in it by nature may be fully developed, and its
destination here on earth fulfilled. Such a justification of nature,—
or rather, let us say, of providence,—is no insignificant motive

for choosing a particular point of view in contemplating the course of the world. For, what avails it, to magnify the glory and wisdom of the creation in the irrational domain of nature, and to recommend it to devout contemplation, if that part of the great display of the supreme wisdom, which presents the end of it all in the history of the human race, is to be viewed as only furnishing perpetual objections to that glory and wisdom? The spectacle of history if thus viewed would compel us to turn away our eyes from it against our will; and the despair of ever finding a perfect rational purpose in its movement, would reduce us to hope for it, if at all, only in another world.

This idea of a universal history is no doubt to a certain extent of an *a priori* character, but it would be a misunderstanding of my object were it imagined that I have any wish to supplant the empirical cultivation of history, or the narration of the actual facts of experience. It is only a thought of what a philosophical mind—which, as such, must be thoroughly versed in history— might be induced to attempt from another standpoint. Besides, the praiseworthy circumstantiality with which our history is now written, may well lead one to raise the question as to how our remote posterity will be able to cope with the burden of history as it will be transmitted to them after a few centuries? They will surely estimate the history of the oldest times, of which the documentary records may have been long lost, only from the point of view of what will interest them; and no doubt this will be what the nations and governments have achieved, or failed to achieve, in the universal world-wide relation. It is well to be giving thought to this relation; and at the same time to draw the attention of ambitious rulers and their servants to the only means by which they can leave an honourable memorial of themselves to latest times. And this may also form a minor motive for attempting to produce such a philosophical history.

2 *Marquis de Condorcet*

While in hiding from Robespierre and the Revolutionary Terror in the winter of 1793-1794, a Girondist politician and minor philosopher of the Enlightenment wrote the first complete history of mankind seen as the progressive evolution of the species from primeval savagery to future universal well-being. Through this single work, Outline of an Historical Picture of the Progress of the Human Mind, *the Marquis de Condorcet (1743-1794) earned the immortality that had eluded him during the first fifty years of his life. His* Outline *was published posthumously in 1795, and it provided the form, as Frank Manuel writes, "in which the eighteenth-century idea of progress was generally assimilated by Western thought." Presented here are the introduction and an excerpt from the chapter on the Tenth Epoch, Condorcet's vision of things to come.*

Man is born with the faculty of receiving sensations, of understanding and distinguishing, in those which he receives, the simple sensations of which they are composed, of retaining, identifying, combining them, of preserving or calling them back to memory, of comparing these combinations, of seizing on what they have in common and what distinguishes them, of attaching signs to all these objects, in order to recognize them better, and to facilitate new combinations.

This faculty is developed in him by the action of things external, that is to say, by the presence of certain compound sensations whose constancy, whether in their identity as a whole or in the laws of their changes, is independent of himself. He exercises it

SOURCE. Marquis de Condorcet, *Esquisse d'un tableau historique des progrès de l'esprit humain*, Paris: Masson, 1822, pp. 1–16 and 262–265. Translated for this book by W. Warren Wagar. Reprinted by permission of Masson & Cie.

also by communicating with individuals similar to himself, and finally by artificial means, which after the first development of this same faculty men succeeded in discovering.

The sensations are accompanied by pleasure and pain, and man has also the faculty of transforming these momentary impressions into durable feelings, whether sweet or painful; of experiencing these feelings at the sight or recollection of the pleasures or pains of other beings capable of sensation. Finally, from this faculty, allied with that of forming and combining ideas, are born the relations of interest and of duty between man and his fellows to which nature herself has decided to attach the most precious portion of our happiness and the most grievous of our woes.

If one limits himself to observing and discerning the general facts and the constant laws which the development of these faculties presents, as regards that which the various individuals of the human species have in common, this science bears the name of Metaphysics.

But if one considers this same development in its results, relative to the mass of individuals who co-exist at the same time in a given space, and if one follows it from generation to generation, it presents then the picture of the progress of the human mind. This progress is subject to the same general laws which are observed in the individual development of our faculties, since it is the result of this development, viewed at the same time in a great number of individuals joined together in society. But the result obtained at each moment depends on that of preceding moments, and influences what will happen in times to come.

This picture is therefore historical, since, subject to perpetual variations, it is formed by the successive observation of human societies in the different epochs through which they have passed. It should present the order of the changes, reveal the influence which each moment exerts on the one that takes its place, and thus show, in the modifications which mankind has undergone, as it renews itself ceaselessly through the immensity of the ages, the path which it has followed, the steps which it has taken toward truth or happiness. These observations on what man has been, on what he is today, will lead in due course to the means of assuring and accelerating the fresh progress for which his nature permits him to hope.

Such is the goal of the work which I have undertaken, of which the result will be to show by reason and by evidence that no limit has been set to the perfection of human faculties; that the perfectibility of man is really indefinite; that the progress of this perfectibility, henceforth independent of every power which might wish to stop it, has no limit other than the duration of the globe on which nature has cast us. No doubt this progress could proceed more rapidly or less, but never will it be retrograde, at least so long as the earth occupies the same place in the system of the universe, and so long as the general laws of this system produce on this globe neither general destruction nor changes which would no longer permit the human race to preserve and employ the same faculties here, and to find here the same resources.

The first state of civilization in which the human race has been observed is that of a sparsely populated society of men making their livelihood from hunting and fishing, familiar only with the crude art of making their weapons and certain household utensils, of building or digging themselves dwellings, but having already a language to express their needs to one another, and a small number of moral ideas, from which they deduce common rules of conduct, living in families, conforming themselves to the general customs which for them take the place of laws, and having even a crude form of government.

We perceive that the uncertainty and the difficulty of providing for his subsistence and the obligatory choice between extreme fatigue and absolute rest, do not leave man that leisure in which, abandoning himself to his ideas, he can enrich his intellect with new combinations. The means of satisfying his needs are by the same token too dependent on luck and the seasons to prompt advantageously the development of an industry with prospects of continued progress; and each individual limits himself to perfecting his personal skill and dexterity.

Thus, the progress of the human species at that time had to be very slow; it could be made only at great intervals, and when it was favored by extraordinary circumstances. Nevertheless, after dependence upon hunting, fishing, or fruits yielded spontaneously by the earth, comes nourishment furnished by animals which man has domesticated and which he knows how to keep and multiply. To these methods next is added a crude sort of agriculture; man is no longer satisfied with the fruits or plants that he happens upon; he learns to store them, to gather them around him, to sow or plant them, and to assist their reproduction by cultivation.

Property which, in the first state, was limited to the animals man killed, to his weapons, his nets, his household utensils, was now extended to include first his flock, and next the land which he cleared and cultivates. With the death of the head, this property naturally passes to his family. Some people have a surplus, which they can keep on hand. If it is a surplus in the absolute sense, it gives rise to new wants; if it occurs in one thing only, while another is lacking, this need suggests the idea of an exchange: from that point, moral relations become complicated and multiply. Greater security, more assured and constant leisure permit meditation or at least regular observation. The custom is introduced, for some individuals, of giving a part of their surplus in exchange for labor, from which they themselves are then freed. There comes into existence, then, a class of men whose time is not absorbed by bodily labor and whose desires exceed their simple needs. Industry awakens; arts already known extend and perfect themselves; facts which chance offers to the observation of man, now more attentive and better trained, facilitate the birth of new arts; the population grows in proportion as the means of subsistence become less hazardous and less precarious; agriculture, which can nourish a greater number of individuals on the same amount of land, replaces the other sources of subsistence; it favors this multiplication, which, in turn, accelerates its progress; the ideas acquired are communicated more rapidly and perpetuate themselves more surely in a society which has become more sedentary, more consolidated, more intimate. Already the dawn of the sciences begins to appear; man shows himself to be separate from the other animal species, and seems no longer limited, like them, to a purely individual perfection.

The more extensive, numerous, and complicated relations which men then form among one another cause them to feel the need

to communicate their ideas to individuals not present, to perpetuate the memory of a fact with more precision than through oral
tradition, to fix the terms of an agreement more surely than
through the memory of witnesses, and to establish, in a manner
less subject to changes, those revered customs by which the members of the same society have agreed to regulate their conduct.

The need then was felt for writing, and it was invented. It
appears that it was at first true painting, followed later by conventional painting, which preserved only the characteristic qualities of objects. Next, by a kind of metaphor analogous to that
already introduced into language, the image of a physical object
expressed moral ideas. The origin of these signs, like that of words,
was bound to be forgotten in the long run; and writing became
the art of attaching a conventional sign to each idea, each word,
and in consequence to each modification of ideas and words.

Now man had a written and a spoken language, each of which
had to be learned and between which it was necessary to establish
a mutual correspondence.

Men of genius, eternal benefactors of humanity, whose names
and even whose countries are buried forever in oblivion, observed
that all the words of a language were only the combinations of a
very limited quantity of elementary articulations, and that the
number of these, although quite limited, sufficed to form a nearly
infinite number of various combinations. They had the imagination to represent by visible signs not the ideas or words to which
they corresponded, but these simple elements of which the words
are composed.

From that time on, alphabetical writing was known; a small
number of signs was adequate to write everything, as a small number of sounds was adequate to say everything. The written language was the same as the spoken; one needed only to know how
to recognize and form these few signs, and this last step assured
forever the progress of the human species.

Perhaps it would be useful today to institute a written language,
reserved exclusively for the sciences, expressing only those combinations of simple ideas found exactly alike in all minds, employed
only for arguments of logical rigor, for precise and determined
processes of the understanding, which would be comprehended

by the men of all countries and translated into all their idioms without, like these, being susceptible of alteration by passing into common usage.

Then, by an odd turn of events, that same type of writing, whose preservation would have served only to prolong ignorance, would become in the hands of the philosopher a useful instrument for the rapid propagation of enlightenment and the perfecting of the scientific method.

It is between this stage of civilization and the one in which we see savage tribes living today that all the peoples whose history has been preserved down to our time are found. Now making fresh progress, now plunging back into ignorance; sometimes carrying on their lives in the middle between these two extremes, or halting at a certain limit; sometimes disappearing from the earth under the conqueror's sword, mingling with the victors, or subsisting in slavery; sometimes, finally, receiving knowledge from a more enlightened people, to transmit it to other nations, these peoples form an unbroken chain between the beginning of historic times and the century in which we live, between the first nations known to us and the peoples of Europe today.

We can thus perceive already three quite distinct parts in the picture which I have set myself to draw.

In the first, where the stories of voyagers show us the state of the human species among the least civilized peoples, we are reduced to guessing by what stages isolated man, or rather, man limited to the amount of association needed for purposes of reproduction, was able to acquire those early accomplishments, highest of which is the use of an articulate language—the most marked quality, and indeed the only one, along with certain more extensive moral ideas and the feeble beginning of social order, which distinguishes man from the animals who live, like himself, in a regular and durable society. Therefore we can have here no guide other than observations of the development of our faculties.

Then, to bring man to the point at which he practices arts, at which the light of the sciences already begins to instruct him, at which finally alphabetical writing is invented, we can add to this first guide the history of the various societies which have been observed in nearly all the intermediate stages, although no one of them can be followed through all the length of time which separates these two great epochs of humanity.

Here, the picture begins to depend in large measure on the series of facts which history has handed down to us; but it is necessary to select them from the history of different peoples, to bring them together and combine them, in order to extract from all this the hypothetical history of a single people and portray its progress.

Since the epoch when alphabetical writing was known in Greece, history is tied to our century, to the present state of the human species in the most enlightened countries of Europe, by an uninterrupted series of facts and observations; and the picture of the course and progress of the human mind has become truly historical. Philosophy has no more guesswork to do, no more hypothetical combinations to form; it suffices to gather together, to order the facts, and to show the useful truths which come to light from their interconnectedness and from their totality.

Only one last picture would then remain to be drawn, that of our hopes, of the progress reserved to future generations, which the constancy of the laws of nature seems to guarantee them. There it would be necessary to show by what degrees that which might appear to us today a chimerical hope may gradually become possible and even easy; why, despite the temporary triumphs of prejudices and the support they receive from the corruption of governments or peoples, the truth alone may win a lasting victory; by what ties nature has indissolubly united the progress of knowledge and the progress of liberty, of virtue, of respect for the natural rights of man; how these only real blessings, so often separated that they have even been thought incompatible, must on the contrary become inseparable, from the moment when knowledge shall have reached a certain level in a great number of nations all at one time, and when it shall have penetrated the whole mass of one great people whose language shall be universally disseminated and whose commercial relations shall embrace all the breadth of the globe. Once this union of blessings is affected throughout the class of enlightened men, from that point they will all be friends of humanity, engaged in hastening in concert its perfection and happiness.

We shall reveal the origins, we shall trace the history of the universal errors which have more or less retarded or suspended the advance of reason; even as much as political events, these have often caused man to turn backwards toward ignorance.

The operations of the understanding which lead us to error, or which keep us there, from the subtle paralogism which can dupe the most enlightened man to the dreams of madness, belong to the theory of the development of our individual faculties no less than the correct method of reasoning or that of discovering truth; and for the same reason, the way in which universal errors are introduced, propagated, transmitted, and perpetuated among peoples, constitutes part of the historical picture of the progress of the human mind. Like the truths which perfect and illuminate it, they are the necessary consequence of its activity, of that disproportion always existing between what it knows, what it desires to know, and what it thinks it needs to know.

One may even observe that, according to the general laws of the development of our faculties, certain prejudices have perforce arisen in each epoch of our progress, which then, however, extend much further than necessary their seductive power or their sway, because men preserve the errors of their childhood, of their country and their century, long after having become familiar with all the truths necessary to destroy them.

And so in all countries, at all times, there exist different prejudices, according to the degree of education of the various classes of men, and according to their professions as well. If the prejudices of the philosophers are detrimental to the fresh progress of truth, those of the less enlightened classes retard the propagation of truths already known; those of certain esteemed or powerful professions raise obstacles thereto: these are the three types of enemies whom reason is obliged to fight unceasingly, and over which it often triumphs only after a long and painful struggle. The history of these conflicts, of the birth, the triumph, and the fall of prejudices, will occupy therefore a large place in this work, and will not be the least important or the least useful part of it.

If there is to exist a science of foreseeing the progress of the human species, of directing and accelerating it, the history of the progress already made must be its principal foundation. No doubt philosophy has been obliged to proscribe that superstition which held in effect that rules of conduct could be found only in the history of past centuries, and truths only in the study of ancient opinion. But should she not include in the same proscription the prejudice which would arrogantly reject the lessons of experience? Without doubt, meditation alone can, by fortunate combinations, lead us to the general truths of the science of man. But if the study of the individuals of the human species is useful to the metaphysician, and to the moralist, why would the study of society be less so to them? Why would it not be useful to the political philosopher? If it is useful to observe the various societies which exist at the same time, to study the relations between them, why would it not be useful to observe them also through the course of time? Supposing even that these observations can be neglected in the pursuit of speculative truths, must this happen when it is a question of putting these truths into practice and of deducing from the science, the art which should be its useful product? Our prejudices, the evils which are the consequences of them—have they not their source in the prejudices of our ancestors? One of the surest means of undeceiving ourselves with regard to the ones, and of forestalling the others, is to elucidate their origins and effects.

Are we at the point where we no longer have to fear either new errors or the return of old ones; where no corrupting institution can be introduced by hypocrisy, and adopted by ignorance or enthusiasm; where no vicious combination can any longer inflict misfortune on a great nation? Would it then be useless to know how peoples have been deceived, corrupted, or plunged into misery?

Everything tells us that we are approaching the epoch of one of the great revolutions of the human race. What can better enlighten us as to what we must expect from it; what can offer us a surer guide to lead us through its turbulence, than the picture of the revolutions which have preceded and prepared it? The present state of knowledge guarantees us that it will be successful; but is this not also on condition that we know how to make use of all our powers? And in order that the happiness which it promises may be bought less dearly, in order that it may spread with greater speed through a larger part of the world, in order that it may be more complete in its effects, do we not need to study, in the history of the human mind, what obstacles remain for us to fear, what means we have of surmounting them?

I shall divide the area that I propose to cover into nine great epochs; and I shall be so bold as to risk, in a tenth, some glances at the future destiny of the human race.

* * *

If man can predict with almost complete assurance the phenomena whose laws he knows; if even when they are not known to him, he can, following past experience, foresee the events of the future with a high degree of probability; why should it be regarded as a chimerical undertaking to draw with a certain verisimilitude the picture of the future destiny of the human species, extrapolating from the pattern of the past? The sole foundation of belief in the natural sciences is the idea that the general laws, known or unknown, which govern the phenomena of the Universe, are necessary and constant; and why should this principle be less true for the development of the intellectual and moral faculties of man than for the other operations of nature? In short, since ideas based on past experience with regard to matters of the same sort are the only rule of conduct of the wisest men, why forbid the philosopher from basing his conjectures on this same foundation, provided that he does not attribute to them a certitude superior to that which can spring from the number, consistency, and exactness of his observations?

Our hopes as to the future state of the human race can be reduced to these three important points: the destruction of inequality among the nations; the progress of equality within nations; finally, the actual perfecting of man. Are all nations one day to approach the civilized state already reached by the peoples most enlightened, most free, most emancipated from prejudices, such as the French and the Anglo-Americans? Is not this immense distance which separates these peoples from the servitude of nations subject to kings, from the barbarism of the African tribes, from the ignorance of savages, destined little by little to vanish? Are there countries on the globe whose inhabitants nature has condemned never to enjoy liberty, never to exercise their reason? Is that difference in knowledge, means, or wealth until now observed in all civilized peoples between the different classes which make up each of them, is that inequality which the early progress of society increased, and so to speak produced, inherent in civilization itself, or is it due to the existing imperfections of social art? May it gradually weaken and give place to that real equality, final goal of social art, which, diminishing even the effects of natural differences in ability, lets remain only so much inequality as may be in the common interest, because it will favor the progress of civilization, of education, and of industry, without entailing dependence, humiliation, or impoverishment? In a word, will men approach that state in which all will have the knowledge necessary to conduct themselves according to their own reason in the common affairs of life, and maintain that reason free from prejudices, knowing full well their rights and exercising them according to their opinion and their conscience; that state in which all will be able, through the development of their faculties, to obtain sure means of providing for their needs; and lastly that state in which stupidity and misery will no longer be anything but accidents, and not the customary condition of a whole portion of society?

Finally, is the human race destined to improve itself, whether by new discoveries in the sciences and arts, and consequently in the means of securing individual well-being and general prosperity; or by progress in the principles of conduct and in practical morality; or, lastly, by the actual perfecting of the intellectual, moral, and physical faculties, which can be just as well the result either of the perfecting of the instruments which increase the intensity or direct the use of these faculties, or the perfecting of our natural organization itself?

In answering these three questions, we shall find in the experience of the past, in the observation of the progress that the sciences and civilization have made thus far, in the analysis of the advance of the human mind and the development of its faculties, the strongest motives for believing that nature has set no limit to our hopes.

3 Auguste Comte

The founder of Positivism and the self-styled "High Priest of Humanity," Auguste Comte (1798-1857), regarded progress not only as a fact of history but also as a law; and from Comte springs the familiar nineteenth-century idea that the central problem of sociology is to discover the law and mechanism of human progress. His own solution, the overarching principle in the six volumes of his Course in Positive Philosophy, *1830-1842, is the law of the three states. A clear exposition of it may be found in the first chapter of the introduction to Harriet Martineau's useful abridgment of the complete work, which she published as a labor of love in 1853.*

A general statement of any system of philosophy may be either a sketch of a doctrine to be established, or a summary of a doctrine already established. If greater value belongs to the last, the first is still important, as characterizing from its origin the subject to be treated. In a case like the present, where the proposed study is vast and hitherto indeterminate, it is especially important that the field of research should be marked out with all possible accuracy. For this purpose, I will glance at the considerations which have originated this work, and which will be fully elaborated in the course of it.

In order to understand the true value and character of the positive philosophy, we must take a brief general view of the pro-

SOURCE. Auguste Comte, *The Positive Philosophy*, translated and abridged by Harriet Martineau, Chicago: Belford, Clarke & Co., pp. 25–28, 32, 34, 35, and 36–37.

gressive course of the human mind, regarded as a whole; for no conception can be understood otherwise than through its history.

Law of Human Progress

From the study of the development of human intelligence, in all directions, and through all times, the discovery arises of a great fundamental law, to which it is necessarily subject, and which has a solid foundation of proof, both in the facts of our organization and in our historical experience. The law is this:—that each of our leading conceptions,—each branch of our knowledge,—passes successively through three different theoretical conditions: the theological, or fictitious; the metaphysical, or abstract; and the scientific, or positive. In other words, the human mind, by its nature, employs in its progress three methods of philosophizing, the character of which is essentially different, and even radically opposed: viz., the theological method, the metaphysical, and the positive. Hence arise three philosophies, or general systems of conceptions on the aggregate of phenomena, each of which excludes the others. The first is the necessary point of departure of the human understanding; and the third is its fixed definitive state. The second is merely a state of transition.

First Stage

In the theological state, the human mind, seeking the essential nature of beings, the first and final causes (the origin and purpose) of all effects,—in short, absolute knowledge,—supposes all phenomena to be produced by the immediate action of supernatural beings.

Second Stage

In the metaphysical state, which is only a modification of the first, the mind supposes, instead of supernatural beings, abstract forces, veritable entities (that is, personified abstractions) inherent in all beings, and capable of producing all phenomena. What is called the explanation of phenomena is, in this stage, a mere reference of each to its proper entity.

Third Stage

In the final, the positive state, the mind has given over the vain search after absolute notions, the origin and destination of the universe, and the causes of phenomena, and applies itself to the study of their laws,—that is, their invariable relations of succession and resemblance. Reasoning and observation, duly combined, are the means of this knowledge. What is now understood when we speak of an explanation of facts is simply the establishment of a connection between single phenomena and some general facts, the number of which continually diminishes with the progress of science.

Ultimate Point of Each

The theological system arrived at the highest perfection of which it is capable when it substituted the providential action of a single Being for the varied operations of the numerous divinities which had been before imagined. In the same way, in the last stage of the metaphysical system, men substitute one great entity (Nature) as the cause of all phenomena, instead of the multitude of entities at first supposed. In the same way, again, the ultimate perfection of the positive system would be (if perfection could be hoped for) to represent all phenomena as particular aspects of a single general fact;—such as gravitation, for instance.

The importance of the working of this general law will be established hereafter. At present, it must suffice to point out some of the grounds of it.

Actual Evidences of the Law

There is no science which, having attained the positive stage, does not bear marks of having passed through the others. Some time since it was (whatever it might be) composed, as we can now perceive, of metaphysical abstractions; and further back in the course of time, it took its form from theological conceptions. We shall have only too much occasion to see, as we proceed, that our most advanced sciences still bear very evident marks of the two earlier periods through which they have passed.

The progress of the individual mind is not only an illustration, but an indirect evidence of that of the general mind. The point of departure of the individual and of the race being the same, the phases of the mind of a man correspond to the epochs of the mind of the race. Now, each of us is aware, if he looks back upon his own history, that he was a theologian in his childhood, a meta-physician in his youth, and a natural philosopher in his manhood. All men who are up to their age can verify this for themselves.

Besides the observation of facts, we have theoretical reasons in support of this law.

Theoretical Evidences

The most important of these reasons arises from the necessity that always exists for some theory to which to refer our facts, combined with the clear impossibility that, at the outset of human knowledge, men could have formed theories out of the observation of facts. All good intellects have repeated, since Bacon's time, that there can be no real knowledge but that which is based on observed facts. This is incontestable, in our present advanced stage; but, if we look back to the primitive stage of human knowledge, we shall see that it must have been otherwise then. If it is true that every theory must be based upon observed facts, it is equally true that facts cannot be observed without the guidance of some theory. Without such guidance, our facts would be desultory and fruitless; we could not retain them; for the most part we could not even perceive them.

Thus, between the necessity of observing facts in order to form a theory, and having a theory in order to observe facts, the human mind would have been entangled in a vicious circle, but for the natural opening afforded by theological conceptions. This is the fundamental reason for the theological character of the primitive philosophy. This necessity is confirmed by the perfect suitability of the theological philosophy to the earliest researches of the human mind. It is remarkable that the most inaccessible questions,—those of the nature of beings, and the origin and purpose of phenomena,—should be the first to occur in a primitive state, while those which are really within our reach are regarded as almost unworthy of serious study. The reason is evident enough: —that experience alone can teach us the measure of our powers; and if men had not begun by an exaggerated estimate of what they can do, they would never have done all that they are capable of. Our organization requires this. At such a period there could have been no reception of a positive philosophy, whose function is to discover the laws of phenomena, and whose leading characteristic it is to regard as interdicted to human reason those sublime mysteries which theology explains, even to their minutest details, with the most attractive facility. It is just so under a practical view of the nature of the researches with which men first occupied themselves. Such inquiries offered the powerful charm of unlimited empire over the external world,—a world destined wholly for our use, and involved in every way with our existence. The theological philosophy, presenting this view, administered exactly the stimulus necessary to incite the human mind to the irksome labour without which it could make no progress. We can now scarcely conceive of such a state of things, our reason having become sufficiently mature to enter upon laborious scientific researches, without needing any such stimulus as wrought upon the imaginations of astrologers and alchemists. We have motive enough in the hope of discovering the laws of phenomena, with a view to the confirmation or rejection of a theory. But it could not be so in the earliest days; and it is to the chimeras of astrology and alchemy that we owe the long series of observations and experiments on which our positive science is based. Kepler felt this on behalf of astronomy, and Berthollet on behalf of chemistry. Thus was a spontaneous philosophy, the theological, the only possible beginning, method, and provisional system, out of which the positive philosophy could grow. It is easy, after this, to perceive how metaphysical methods and doctrines must have afforded the means of transition from the one to the other.

The human understanding, slow in its advance, could not step at once from the theological into the positive philosophy. The two are so radically opposed, that an intermediate system of conceptions has been necessary to render the transition possible. It is only in doing this, that metaphysical conceptions have any utility whatever. In contemplating phenomena, men substitute for supernatural direction a corresponding entity. This entity may have been supposed to be derived from the supernatural action; but it is more easily lost sight of, leaving attention free for the facts themselves, till, at length, metaphysical agents have ceased to be anything more than the abstract names of phenomena. It is not easy to say by what other process than this our minds could have passed from supernatural considerations to natural; from the theological system to the positive.

* * *

We must now glance at the chief advantages which must be derived, on behalf of human progression, from the study of [the Positive Philosophy]. Of these advantages, four may be especially pointed out.

I. The study of the Positive Philosophy affords the only rational means of exhibiting the logical laws of the human mind, which have hitherto been sought by unfit methods.

II. The second effect of the Positive Philosophy, an effect not less important and far more urgently wanted, will be to regenerate Education.

The best minds are agreed that our European education, still essentially theological, metaphysical, and literary, must be superseded by a Positive training, conformable to our time and needs. Even the governments of our day have shared, where they have not originated, the attempts to establish positive instruction; and this is a striking indication of the prevalent sense of what is wanted.

III. The same special study of scientific generalities must also aid the progress of the respective positive sciences: and this constitutes our third head of advantages.

IV. The Positive Philosophy offers the only solid basis for that Social Reorganization which must succeed the critical condition in which the most civilized nations are now living.

It can not be necessary to prove to anybody who reads this work that Ideas govern the world, or throw it into chaos; in other words, that all social mechanism rests upon Opinions. The great political and moral crisis that societies are now undergoing is shown by a rigid analysis to arise out of intellectual anarchy. While stability in fundamental maxims is the first condition of genuine social order, we are suffering under an utter disagreement which may be called universal. Till a certain number of general ideas can be acknowledged as a rallying-point of social doctrine, the nations will remain in a revolutionary state, whatever palliatives may be devised; and their institutions can be only provisional. But whenever the necessary agreement on first principles can be obtained, appropriate institutions will issue from them, without shock or resistance; for the causes of disorder will have been arrested by the mere fact of the agreement. It is in this direction that those must look who desire a natural and regular, a normal state of society.

Now, the existing disorder is abundantly accounted for by the existence, all at once, of three incompatible philosophies—the theological, the metaphysical, and the positive. Any one of these might alone secure some sort of social order; but while the three co-exist, it is impossible for us to understand one another upon any essential point whatever. If this is true, we have only to ascertain which of the philosophies must, in the nature of things, prevail; and, this ascertained, every man, whatever may have been his former views, can not but concur in its triumph. The problem once recognised, can not remain long unsolved; for all considerations whatever point to the Positive Philosophy as the one destined to prevail. It alone has been advancing during a course of centuries, throughout which the others have been declining. The fact is incontestable. Some may deplore it, but none can destroy it, nor therefore neglect it but under penalty of being betrayed by illusory speculations. This general revolution of the human mind is nearly accomplished. We have only to complete the Positive Philosophy by bringing Social phenomena within its comprehension, and afterward consolidating the whole into one body of homogeneous doctrine. The marked preference which almost all minds, from the highest to the commonest, accord to positive knowledge over vague and mystical conceptions, is a pledge of what the reception of this philosophy will be when it has acquired the only quality that it now wants—a character of due generality. When it has become complete, its supremacy will take place spontaneously, and will re-establish order throughout society. There is, at present, no conflict but between the theological and the metaphysical philosophies. They are contending for the task of reorganizing society; but it is a work too mighty for either of them. The positive philosophy has hitherto intervened only to examine both, and both are abundantly discredited by the process.

It is time now to be doing something more effective, without wasting our forces in needless controversy. It is time to complete the vast intellectual operation begun by Bacon, Descartes, and Galileo, by constructing the system of general ideas which must henceforth prevail among the human race. This is the way to put an end to the revolutionary crisis which is tormenting the civilized nations of the world.

PART FOUR

Progress and Conflict

1 Karl Marx and Friedrich Engels

Down to the middle of the nineteenth century, exponents of the idea of progress explained the amelioration of mankind largely in terms of the progress of knowledge, and especially of science. In the latter part of the nineteenth century, the emphasis often fell on struggle—whether of individuals, classes, nations, or races—as the chief agent of human betterment. The most important representatives of late nineteenth-century conflict theory from our present perspective are Karl Marx (1818-1883) and Friedrich Engels (1820-1895). Marxism is not simply a program for socialist revolution or an unsympathetic analysis of capitalism: it also embodies a complete philosophy of history seen as the inevitable progress of humanity through equally inevitable class conflict. Three selections appear below from the writings of Marx and Engels: brief excerpts from The Manifesto of the Communist Party, *1848; from Marx's* A Contribution to the Critique of Political Economy, *1859; and from Engels's* Socialism: Utopian and Scientific, *1880.*

A. THE COMMUNIST MANIFESTO (Marx and Engels)

Hitherto every form of society has been based, as we have already seen, on the antagonism of oppressing and oppressed classes. But in order to oppress a class certain conditions must be assured to it under which it can, at least, continue its slavish existence. The serf, in the period of serfdom, raised himself to membership in the commune, just as the petty bourgeois, under the yoke of feudal absolutism, managed to develop into a bourgeois. The modern laborer, on the contrary, instead of rising with the progress of industry, sinks deeper and deeper below the conditions of exist-

SOURCE. Lewis S. Feuer, editor, Marx and Engels, *Basic Writings on Politics and Philosophy*, New York: Anchor Books, Inc., 1959, pp. 19-20, 27-29, 43-44, and 105-109. Reprinted by permission of Lewis S. Feuer.

ence of his own class. He becomes a pauper, and pauperism develops more rapidly than population and wealth. And here it becomes evident that the bourgeoisie is unfit any longer to be the ruling class in society, and to impose its conditions of existence upon society as an overriding law. It is unfit to rule because it is incompetent to assure an existence to its slave within his slavery, because it cannot help letting him sink into such a state that it has to feed him instead of being fed by him. Society can no longer live under this bourgeoisie: in other words, its existence is no longer compatible with society.

The essential condition for the existence, and for the sway of the bourgeois class, is the formation and augmentation of capital; the condition for capital is wage labor. Wage labor rests exclusively on competition between the laborers. The advance of industry, whose involuntary promoter is the bourgeoisie, replaces the isolation of the laborers, due to competition, by their revolutionary combination, due to association. The development of modern industry, therefore, cuts from under its feet the very foundation on which the bourgeoisie produces and appropriates products. What the bourgeoisie, therefore, produces, above all, is its own gravediggers. Its fall and the victory of the proletariat are equally inevitable.

We have seen above that the first step in the revolution by the working class is to raise the proletariat to the position of ruling class, to win the battle of democracy.

The proletariat will use its political supremacy to wrest, by degrees, all capital from the bourgeoisie, to centralize all instruments of production in the hands of the state, i.e., of the proletariat organized as the ruling class, and to increase the total of productive forces as rapidly as possible.

Of course, in the beginning this cannot be effected except by means of despotic inroads on the rights of property and on the conditions of bourgeois production; by means of measures, therefore, which appear economically insufficient and untenable, but which, in the course of the movement, outstrip themselves, necessitate further inroads upon the old social order, and are unavoidable as a means of entirely revolutionizing the mode of production.

These measures will of course be different in different countries. Nevertheless, in the most advanced countries the following will be pretty generally applicable:

1. Abolition of property in land and application of all rents of land to public purposes.
2. A heavy progressive or graduated income tax.
3. Abolition of all right of inheritance.
4. Confiscation of the property of all emigrants and rebels.
5. Centralization of credit in the hands of the state, by means of a national bank with state capital and an exclusive monopoly.
6. Centralization of the means of communication and transport in the hands of the state.
7. Extension of factories and instruments of production owned by the state; the bringing into cultivation of wastelands, and the improvement of the soil generally in accordance with a common plan.
8. Equal liability of all to labor. Establishment of industrial armies, especially for agriculture.
9. Combination of agriculture with manufacturing industries; gradual abolition of the distinction between town and country, by a more equable distribution of the population over the country.
10. Free education for all children in public schools. Abolition of children's factory labor in its present form. Combination of education with industrial production, etc.

When, in the course of development, class distinctions have disappeared and all production has been concentrated in the hands of a vast association of the whole nation, the public power will lose its political character. Political power, properly so called, is merely the organized power of one class for oppressing another. If the proletariat during its contest with the bourgeoisie is compelled, by the force of circumstances, to organize itself as a class, if, by means of a revolution, it makes itself the ruling class and, as such, sweeps away by force the old conditions of production, then it will, along with these conditions, have swept away the conditions for the existence of class antagonisms and of classes generally, and will thereby have abolished its own supremacy as a class.

In place of the old bourgeois society, with its classes and class antagonisms, we shall have an association in which the free development of each is the condition for the free development of all.

B.   A CONTRIBUTION TO THE CRITIQUE OF POLITICAL ECONOMY (Marx)

I was led by my studies to the conclusion that legal relations as well as forms of state could be neither understood by themselves nor explained by the so-called general progress of the human mind, but that they are rooted in the material conditions of life, which are summed up by Hegel after the fashion of the English and French of the eighteenth century under the name "civil society"; the anatomy of that civil society is to be sought in political economy. The study of the latter, which I had taken up in Paris, I continued at Brussels, whither I immigrated on account of an order of expulsion issued by Mr. Guizot. The general conclusion at which I arrived and which, once reached, continued to serve as the leading thread in my studies may be briefly summed up as follows: In the social production which men carry on they enter into definite relations that are indispensable and independent of their will; these relations of production correspond to a definite stage of development of their material powers of production. The sum total of these relations of production constitutes the economic structure of society—the real foundation, on which rise legal and political superstructures and to which correspond definite forms of social consciousness. The mode of production in material life determines the general character of the social, political, and spiritual processes of life. It is not the consciousness of men that determines their existence, but, on the contrary, their social existence determines their consciousness. At a certain stage of their development the material forces of production in society come into conflict with the existing relations of production, or—what is but a legal expression for the same thing —with the property relations within which they had been at work before. From forms of development of the forces of production these relations turn into their fetters. Then comes the period of social revolution. With the change of the economic foundation the entire immense superstructure is more or less rapidly trans-formed. In considering such transformations the distinction should always be made between the material transformation of the eco-nomic conditions of production, which can be determined with the precision of natural science, and the legal, political, religious, aesthetic, or philosophic—in short, ideological—forms in which men become conscious of this conflict and fight it out. Just as our opinion of an individual is not based on what he thinks of himself, so can we not judge such a period of transformation by its own consciousness; on the contrary, this consciousness must rather be explained from the contradictions of material life, from the existing conflict between the social forces of production and the relations of production. No social order ever disappears before all the productive forces for which there is room in it have been developed, and new, higher relations of production never appear before the material conditions of their existence have matured in the womb of the old society. Therefore mankind always takes up only such problems as it can solve, since, looking at the mat-ter more closely, we will always find that the problem itself arises only when the material conditions necessary for its solution already exist or are at least in the process of formation. In broad outlines we can designate the Asiatic, the ancient, the feudal, and the modern bourgeois methods of production as so many epochs in the progress of the economic formation of society. The bour-geois relations of production are the last antagonistic form of the social process of production—antagonistic not in the sense of individual antagonism, but of one arising from conditions sur-rounding the life of individuals in society; at the same time the productive forces developing in the womb of bourgeois society create the material conditions for the solution of that antagonism. This social formation constitutes, therefore, the closing chapter of the prehistoric stage of human society.

C. SOCIALISM: UTOPIAN AND SCIENTIFIC (Engels)

While the capitalist mode of production more and more com-pletely transforms the great majority of the population into proletarians, it creates the power which, under penalty of its own destruction, is forced to accomplish this revolution. While it forces on more and more the transformation of the vast means of production, already socialized, into state property, it shows itself the way to accomplishing this revolution. The *proletariat seizes political power and turns the means of production into state property.*

But in doing this it abolishes itself as proletariat, abolishes all class distinctions and class antagonisms, abolishes also the state as state. Society thus far, based upon class antagonisms, has had need of the state. That is, of an organization of the particular class which was *pro tempore* the exploiting class, an organization for the purpose of preventing any interference from without with the existing conditions of production, and, therefore, especially for the purpose of forcibly keeping the exploited classes in the condition of oppression corresponding with the given mode of production (slavery, serfdom, wage labor). The state was the official representative of society as a whole; the gathering of it together into a visible embodiment. But it was this only in so far as it was the state of that class which itself represented, for the time being, society as a whole: in ancient times, the state of slave-owning citizens; in the Middle Ages, the feudal lords; in our own time, the bourgeoisie. When at last it becomes the real representative of the whole of society it renders itself unnecessary. As soon as there is no longer any social class to be held in subjection, as soon as class rule and the individual struggle for existence based upon our present anarchy in production, with the collisions and excesses arising from these, are removed, nothing more remains to be repressed, and a special repressive force, a state, is no longer necessary. The first act by virtue of which the state really constitutes itself the representative of the whole of society—the taking possession of the means of production in the name of society— this is, at the same time, its last independent act as a state. State interference in social relations becomes, in one domain after another, superfluous, and then dies out of itself; the government of persons is replaced by the administration of things, and by the conduct of processes of production. The state is not "abolished." *It dies out.* This gives the measure of the value of the phrase "*a*

free state," both as to its justifiable use at times by agitators and as
to its ultimate scientific insufficiency, and also of the demands
of the so-called anarchists for the abolition of the state out of hand.

Since the historical appearance of the capitalist mode of production, the appropriation by society of all the means of production has often been dreamed of, more or less vaguely, by individuals as well as by sects, as the ideal of the future. But it could
become possible, could become a historical necessity, only when
the actual conditions for its realization were there. Like every
other social advance, it becomes practicable not by men understanding that the existence of classes is in contradiction to justice,
equality, etc., not by the mere willingness to abolish these classes,
but by virtue of certain new economic conditions. The separation
of society into an exploiting and an exploited class, a ruling and
an oppressed class, was the necesary consequence of the deficient
and restricted development of production in former times. So
long as the total social labor yields only a produce which but
slightly exceeds that barely necessary for the existence of all; so
long, therefore, as labor engages all or almost all the time of the
great majority of the members of society—so long, of necessity,
this society is divided into classes. Side by side with the great
majority, exclusively bond slaves to labor, arises a class freed from
directly productive labor, which looks after the general affairs of
society: the direction of labor, state business, law, science, art,
etc. It is, therefore, the law of division of labor that lies at the
basis of the division into classes. But this does not prevent this
division into classes from being carried out by means of violence
and robbery, trickery and fraud. It does not prevent the ruling
class, once having the upper hand, from consolidating its power
at the expense of the working class, from turning its social leadership into an intensified exploitation of the masses.

But if, upon this showing, division into classes has a certain
historical justification, it has this only for a given period, only
under given social conditions. It was based upon the insufficiency
of production. It will be swept away by the complete development of modern productive forces. And, in fact, the abolition
of classes in society presupposes a degree of historical evolution

at which the existence not simply of this or that particular ruling class, but of any ruling class at all, and, therefore, the existence of class distinction itself, has become an anachronism. It presupposes, therefore, the development of production carried out to a degree at which appropriation of the means of production and of the products, and, with this, of political domination, of the monopoly of culture, and of intellectual leadership by a particular class of society, has become not only superfluous but economically, politically, intellectually a hindrance to development.

This point is now reached. Their political and intellectual bankruptcy is scarcely any longer a secret to the bourgeoisie themselves. Their economic bankruptcy recurs regularly every ten years. In every crisis society is suffocated beneath the weight of its own productive forces and products, which it cannot use, and stands helpless, face to face with the absurd contradiction that the producers have nothing to consume because consumers are wanting. The expansive force of the means of production bursts the bonds that the capitalist mode of production imposed upon them. Their deliverance from these bonds is the one precondition for an unbroken, constantly accelerated development of the productive forces, and therewith for a practically unlimited increase of production itself. Nor is this all. The socialized appropriation of the means of production does away not only with the present artificial restrictions upon production, but also with the positive waste and devastation of productive forces and products that are at the present time the inevitable concomitants of production, and that reach their height in the crises. Further, it sets free for the community at large a mass of means of production and of products by doing away with the senseless extravagance of the ruling classes of today and their political representatives. The possibility of securing for every member of society, by means of socialized production, an existence not only fully sufficient materially, and becoming day by day fuller, but an existence guaranteeing to all the free development and exercise of their physical and mental faculties—this possibility is now for the first time here, but *it is here.*[1]

[1] A few figures may serve to give an approximate idea of the enormous expansive force of the modern means of production, even under capitalist

With the seizing of the means of production by society, production of commodities is done away with, and, simultaneously, the mastery of the product over the producer. Anarchy in social production is replaced by systematic, definite organization. The struggle for individual existence disappears. Then for the first time man, in a certain sense, is finally marked off from the rest of the animal kingdom and emerges from mere animal conditions of existence into really human ones. The whole sphere of the conditions of life which environ man, and which have hitherto ruled man, now comes under the dominion and control of man, who for the first time becomes the real, conscious lord of nature because he has now become master of his own social organization. The laws of his own social action, hitherto standing face to face with man as laws of nature foreign to and dominating him, will now be used with full understanding, and so mastered by him. Man's own social organization, hitherto confronting him as a necessity imposed by nature and history, now becomes the result of his own free action. The extraneous objective forces that have hitherto governed history pass under the control of man himself. Only from that time will man himself, more and more consciously, make his own history—only from that time will the social causes set in movement by him have, in the main and in a constantly growing measure, the results intended by him. It is the ascent of man from the kingdom of necessity to the kingdom of freedom.

pressure. According to Mr. Giffen, the total wealth of Great Britain and Ireland amounted, in round numbers, in

$$1814 \text{ to } £2,200,000,000,$$
$$1865 \text{ to } £6,100,000,000,$$
$$1875 \text{ to } £8,500,000,000.$$

As an instance of the squandering of means of production and of products during a crisis the total loss in the German iron industry alone, in the crisis 1873–78, was given at the Second German Industrial Congress (Berlin, February 21, 1878) as £22,750,000.

2 Karl Pearson

A more typical and more conventional philosophy of progress through struggle than Marxism in the second half of the nineteenth century is illustrated here by excerpts from a lecture given in 1900 in Newcastle by Karl Pearson (1857-1936), then Professor of Applied Mathematics at the University of London, and, after 1911, director of its Francis Galton Laboratory for National Eugenics. He argues, on Darwinian premises, that mankind achieves progress chiefly through the military and commercial rivalry of nations. The war referred to in the first paragraph below is the Boer War in South Africa, which had begun in October, 1899, and still had more than a year to run at the time Pearson was giving his address.

It may be as well now to sum up my position as far as I have yet developed it. I have asked you to look upon the nation as an organized whole in continual struggle with other nations, whether by force of arms or by force of trade and economic processes. I have asked you to look upon this struggle of either kind as a not wholly bad thing; it is the source of human progress throughout the world's history. But if a nation is to maintain its position in this struggle, it must be fully provided with trained brains in every department of national activity, from the government to the factory, and have, if possible, a *reserve of brain and physique* to fall back upon in times of national crisis. Recent events in our commercial as well as in our military experience have led some to doubt whether our supply of trained brains is sufficient, or, at any rate, whether it is available in the right place at the right

SOURCE. Karl Pearson, *National Life from the Standpoint of Science*, London: Black, 1901, pp. 41–51 and 60–62. Reprinted by permission of A. & C. Black Ltd.

moment. Those presumably who hold that the brains are forthcoming have raised the cry of technical instruction, which is to be a remedy for our commercial difficulties. I have little doubt that when this war is finished the cry of military instruction will be raised for our army difficulties. In the latter as in the former case large sums of money will no doubt be demanded for equipment. But I have endeavoured to indicate that there are two preliminary matters to be considered. First, are we quite certain that we have a reserve of brain power ready to be trained? We have to remember that man is subject to the universal law of inheritance, and that a dearth of capacity may arise if we recruit our society from the inferior and not the better stock. If any social opinions or class prejudices tamper with the fertility of the better stocks, then the national character will take but a few generations to be seriously modified. The pressure of population should always tend to push brains and physique into occupations where they are not a primary necessity, for in this way a reserve is formed for the times of national crisis. Such a reserve can always be formed by filling up with men of our own kith and kin the waste lands of the earth, even at the expense of an inferior race of inhabitants. Yet if we grant that our nation has a full supply of brains both in action and in reserve, it is not knowledge in the first place, but intellectual training, which is requisite. We want the master-scout to teach men to observe and reason on their observations, and the equipment of the scout, the actual knowledge of facts and processes, is a minor matter.

You will see that my view—and I think it may be called the scientific view of a nation—is that of an organized whole, kept up to a high pitch of internal efficiency by insuring that its numbers are substantially recruited from the better stocks, and kept up to a high pitch of external efficiency by contest, chiefly by way of war with inferior races, and with equal races by the struggle for trade-routes and for the sources of raw material and of food supply. This is the natural history view of mankind, and I do not think you can in its main features subvert it. Some of you may refuse to acknowledge it, but you cannot really study history and refuse to see its force. Some of you may realize it, and then despair of life; you may decline to admit any glory in a world where the superior race must either eject the inferior, or, mixing with it or even living alongside it, degenerate itself. What beauty can there be when the battle is to the stronger, and the weaker must suffer in the struggle of nations and in the struggle of individual men? You may say: Let us cease to struggle, let us leave the lands of the world to the races that cannot profit by them to the full, let us cease to compete in the markets of the world. Well, we could do it, if we were a small nation living on the produce of our own soil, and a soil so worthless that no other race envied it and sought to appropriate it. We should cease to advance; but then we should naturally give up progress as a good which comes through suffering. I say it is possible for a small rural community to stand apart from the world-contest and to stagnate, if no more powerful nation wants its possessions.

But are we such a community? Is it not a fact that the daily bread of our millions of workers depends on their having somebody to work for? that if we give up the contest for trade-routes and for free markets and for waste lands, we indirectly give up our food-supply? Is it not a fact that our strength depends on these and upon our colonies, and that our colonies have been won by the ejection of inferior races, and are maintained against equal races only by respect for their and our present power? If war or competition lessen the China trade, if a bad harvest or a flood check the import of Egyptian or American cotton, it is the Lancashire operative who feels the pinch. The day when we cease to hold our own among the nations will be the day of catastrophe for our workers at home. We could return to the condition of medieval England, to the condition of Norway or Denmark, but only by a process of intense selection, reducing our millions in a manner which the imagination refuses to contemplate. Being as we are, we cannot give up the struggle, and the moment dearth of ability, the want of brains and physique in the right place, leads to serious defeat, our catastrophe will come. That is the vision which depressed thoughtful men at the beginning of this year; that is the dread which must be ever in the mind of the true statesman when he seeks, on the one hand, to curb the rash venture which may overstrain our power, and on the other hand, to maintain our right to work the unutilized resources of earth, be they in Africa or in Asia.

Struggle of race against race, and of man against man—if this be the scientific view of life, the basis of human progress—how have human love and sympathy come to play such a great part in the world? Here, again, I think science has something to say, although the earlier interpreters of evolution rather obscured it. They painted evolution as the survival of the fittest *individual*, and spoke of his struggle against his *fellows*.

But this is not the only form of selection at work; it is often quite the least effective phase of the contest. Consciously or unconsciously, one type of life is fighting against a second type, and all life is struggling with its physical environment. The safety of a gregarious animal—and man is essentially such—depends upon the intensity with which the social instinct has been developed. The stability of a race depends entirely on the extent to which the social feelings have got a real hold on it. The race, which allows the physically or mentally stronger Tom to make the existence of the somewhat inferior Jack impossible, will never succeed when it comes into contest with a second race. Jack has no interests in common with Tom; the oppressed will hardly get worse terms from a new master. That is why no strong and permanent civilization can be built upon slave labour, why an inferior race doing menial labour for a superior race can give no stable community; that is why we shall never have a healthy social state in South Africa until the white man replaces the dark in the fields and in the mines, and the Kaffir is pushed back towards the equator. The nation organized for the struggle must be a *homogeneous* whole, not a mixture of superior and inferior races. For this reason every new land we colonize with white men is a source of strength; every land of coloured men we simply rule may be needful as a source of food and mineral wealth, but it is not an element of stability to our community, and must ever be regarded with grave anxiety by our statesmen.

This need for homogeneity in a nation may be pushed further. You must not have class differences and wealth differences and education differences so great within the community that you lose the sense of common interest, and feel only the pressure of the struggle of man against man. No tribe of men can work together unless the tribal interest dominates the personal and individual interest at all points where they come into conflict. The struggle among primitive man of tribe against tribe evolved the social instinct. The tribe with the greater social feeling survived; we have to thank the struggle for existence for first making man gregarious, and then intensifying, stage by stage, the social feeling. Such is the scientific account of the origin of our social instincts; and if you come to analyze it such is the origin of what we term morality; morality is only the developed form of the tribal habit, the custom of acting in a certain way towards our fellows, upon which the very safety of the tribe originally depended. Philosophies may be invented, the supersensuous appealed to, in order to increase the sanctions on social or moral conduct; but the natural history of morality begins with the kin, spreads to the tribe, to the nation, to allied races, and ultimately to inferior races and lower types of life, but ever with decreasing intensity. The demands upon the spirit of self-sacrifice which can be made by our kin, by our countrymen, by Europeans, by Chinamen, by Negroes, and by Kaffirs, by animals, may not be clearly defined; but, on the average, they admit of rough graduation, and we find in practice, whatever be our fine philosophies, that the instinct to self-sacrifice wanes as we go down in the scale.

The man who tells us that he feels to all men alike, that he has no sense of kinship, that he has no patriotic sentiment, that he loves the Kaffir as he loves his brother, is probably deceiving himself. If he is not, then all we can say is that a nation of such men, or even a nation with a large minority of such men, will not stand for many generations; it cannot survive in the struggle of the nations, it cannot be a factor in the contest upon which human progress ultimately depends. The national spirit is not a thing to be ashamed of, as the educated man seems occasionally to hold. If that spirit be the mere excrescence of the music-hall, or an ignorant assertion of superiority to the foreigner, it may be ridiculous, it may even be nationally dangerous; but if the national spirit takes the form of a strong feeling of the importance of organizing the nation as a whole, of making its social and

economic conditions such that it is able to do its work in the
world and meet its fellows without hesitation in the field and in
the market, then it seems to me a wholly good spirit—indeed,
one of the highest forms of social, that is, moral instinct.

*   *   *

I have endeavoured to place before you a few of the problems
which, it seems to me, arise from a consideration of some of our
recent difficulties in war and in trade. Science is not a dogma; it
has no infallible popes to pronounce authoritatively what its teaching is. I can only say how it seems to one individual scientific
worker that the doctrine of evolution applies to the history of
nations. My interpretation may be wrong, but of the true method
I am sure: a community of men is as subject as a community of
ants or as a herd of buffaloes to the laws which rule all organic
nature. We cannot escape from them; it serves no purpose to
protest at what some term their cruelty and their bloodthirstiness.
We can only study these laws, recognise what of gain they have
brought to man, and urge the statesman and the thinker to regard
and use them, as the engineer and inventor regard and then turn
to human profit the equally unchangeable laws of physical nature.

The origin of the world and the purport of life are mysteries
alike to the poet, the theologian, and the man of science. One
who has stood somewhat as the mediator between the three ad-
mitted the mystery, saw the cruelty of natural processes when
judged from the relative standpoint of man, but found therein
an undefinable "tendency towards righteousness." If by righteousness he meant wider human sympathies, intenser social instincts,
keener pity, and clearer principles of conduct, then I believe that
tendency, that continual progress of mankind, is the scarcely
recognised outcome of the bitter struggle of race with race, the
result of man, like all other life, being subject to the stern law
of the survival of the fitter, to the victory of the physically and
mentally better organized. Mankind as a whole, like the individual
man, advances through pain and suffering only. The path of
progress is strewn with the wreck of nations; traces are everywhere to be seen of the hecatombs of inferior races, and of victims

who found not the narrow way to the greater perfection. Yet these dead peoples are, in very truth, the stepping-stones on which mankind has arisen to the higher intellectual and deeper emotional life of to-day.

3   T. H. Huxley

Not all late nineteenth-century Darwinists agreed with the notion that progress in nature and in history came about principally through internecine conflict. Darwin's most gifted champion and popularizer in Britain, T.H. Huxley (1825-1895), the grandfather of both Aldous and Sir Julian Huxley, was among the dissenters. He also firmly rejected the hope that mankind could ever literally achieve perfection and the belief that progress was inevitable. But, for all that, he remained a child of the progressivist tradition, as the reader may gather from these passages drawn from an essay written in 1894. Huxley even preserved significant functions for struggle in his philosophy of human evolution, a point often overlooked by commentators.

Under the preceding heads, I have endeavoured to represent in broad, but I hope faithful, outlines the essential features of the state of nature and of that cosmic process of which it is the outcome, so far as was needful for my argument; I have contrasted with the state of nature the state of art, produced by human intelligence and energy, as it is exemplified by a garden; and I have shown that the state of art, here and elsewhere, can be maintained only by the constant counteraction of the hostile influences of the state of nature. Further, I have pointed out that the

SOURCE. T. H. Huxley, "Prologomena" from *Evolution and Ethics*, New York: Appleton, 1896, pp. 33–37 and 43–45. Reprinted by permission of Appleton-Century-Crofts.

'horticultural process' which thus sets itself against the 'cosmic process' is opposed to the latter in principle, in so far as it tends to arrest the struggle for existence, by restraining the multiplication which is one of the chief causes of that struggle, and by creating artificial conditions of life, better adapted to the cultivated plants than are the conditions of the state of nature. And I have dwelt upon the fact that, though the progressive modification, which is the consequence of the struggle for existence in the state of nature, is at an end, such modification may still be effected by that selection, in view of an ideal of usefulness, or of pleasantness, to man, of which the state of nature knows nothing.

I have proceeded to show that a colony, set down in a country in the state of nature, presents close analogies with a garden; and I have indicated the course of action which an administrator, able and willing to carry out horticultural principles, would adopt, in order to secure the success of such a newly formed polity, supposing it to be capable of indefinite expansion. In the contrary case, I have shown that difficulties must arise; that the unlimited increase of the population over a limited area must, sooner or later, reintroduce into the colony that struggle for the means of existence between the colonists, which it was the primary object of the administrator to exclude, insomuch as it is fatal to the mutual peace which is the prime condition of the union of men in society.

I have briefly described the nature of the only radical cure, known to me, for the disease which would thus threaten the existence of the colony; and, however regretfully, I have been obliged to admit that this rigorously scientific method of applying the principles of evolution to human society hardly comes within the region of practical politics; not for want of will on the part of a great many people; but because, for one reason, there is no hope that mere human beings will ever possess enough intelligence to select the fittest. And I have adduced other grounds for arriving at the same conclusion.

I have pointed out that human society took its rise in the organic necessities expressed by imitation and by the sympathetic emotions; and that, in the struggle for existence with the state of nature and with other societies, as part of it, those in which men were thus led to close co-operation had a great advantage.[1] But, since each man retained more or less of the faculties common to all the rest, and especially a full share of the desire for unlimited self-gratification, the struggle for existence within society could only be gradually eliminated. So long as any of it remained, society continued to be an imperfect instrument of the struggle for existence and, consequently, was improvable by the selective influence of that struggle. Other things being alike, the tribe of savages in which order was best maintained; in which there was most security within the tribe and the most loyal mutual support outside it, would be the survivors.

I have termed this gradual strengthening of the social bond, which, though it arrests the struggle for existence inside society, up to a certain point improves the chances of society, as a corporate whole, in the cosmic struggle—the ethical process. I have endeavoured to show that, when the ethical process has advanced so far as to secure every member of the society in the possession of the means of existence, the struggle for existence, as between man and man, within that society is, *ipso facto*, at an end. And, as it is undeniable that the most highly civilized societies have substantially reached this position, it follows that, so far as they are concerned, the struggle for existence can play no important part within them.[2] In other words, the kind of evolution which is brought about in the state of nature cannot take place.

I have further shown cause for the belief that direct selection, after the fashion of the horticulturist and the breeder, neither has played, nor can play, any important part in the evolution of society; apart from other reasons, because I do not see how such selection could be practised without a serious weakening, it may be the destruction, of the bonds which hold society together. It strikes me that men who are accustomed to contemplate the active or passive extirpation of the weak, the unfortunate, and

---

[1] *Collected Essays,* vol. v, Prologue, p. 52.

[2] Whether the struggle for existence with the state of nature and with other societies, so far as they stand in the relation of the state of nature with it, exerts a selective influence upon modern society, and in what direction, are questions not easy to answer. The problem of the effect of military and industrial warfare upon those who wage it is very complicated.

the superfluous; who justify that conduct on the ground that it has the sanction of the cosmic process, and is the only way of ensuring the progress of the race; who, if they are consistent, must rank medicine among the black arts and count the physician a mischievous preserver of the unfit; on whose matrimonial undertakings the principles of the stud have the chief influence; whose whole lives, therefore, are an education in the noble art of suppressing natural affection and sympathy, are not likely to have any large stock of these commodities left. But, without them, there is no conscience, nor any restraint on the conduct of men, except the calculation of self-interest, the balancing of certain present gratifications against doubtful future pains; and experience tells us how much that is worth. Every day, we see firm believers in the hell of the theologians commit acts by which, as they believe when cool, they risk eternal punishment; while they hold back from those which are opposed to the sympathies of their associates.

* * *

To return, once more, to the parallel of horticulture. In the modern world, the gardening of men by themselves is practically restricted to the performance, not of selection, but of that other function of the gardener, the creation of conditions more favourable than those of the state of nature; to the end of facilitating the free expansion of the innate faculties of the citizen, so far as it is consistent with the general good. And the business of the moral and political philosopher appears to me to be the ascertainment, by the same method of observation, experiment, and ratiocination, as is practised in other kinds of scientific work, of the course of conduct which will best conduce to that end.

But, supposing this course of conduct to be scientifically determined and carefully followed out, it cannot put an end to the struggle for existence in the state of nature; and it will not so much as tend, in any way, to the adaptation of man to that state. Even should the whole human race be absorbed in one vast polity, within which "absolute political justice" reigns, the struggle for existence with the state of nature outside it, and the tendency to the return of the struggle within, in consequence of over-multiplication, will remain; and, unless men's inheritance from the ancestors who fought a good fight in the state of nature, their dose of original sin, is rooted out by some method at present unrevealed, at any rate to disbelievers in supernaturalism, every child born into the world will still bring with him the instinct of unlimited self-assertion. He will have to learn the lesson of self-restraint and renunciation. But the practice of self-restraint and renunciation is not happiness, though it may be something much better.

That man, as a "political animal," is susceptible of a vast amount of improvement, by education, by instruction, and by the application of his intelligence to the adaptation of the conditions of life to his higher needs, I entertain not the slightest doubt. But, so long as he remains liable to error, intellectual or moral; so long as he is compelled to be perpetually on guard against the cosmic forces, whose ends are not his ends, without and within himself; so long as he is haunted by inexpugnable memories and hopeless aspirations; so long as the recognition of his intellectual limitations forces him to acknowledge his incapacity to penetrate the mystery of existence; the prospect of attaining untroubled happiness, or of a state which can, even remotely, deserve the title of perfection, appears to me to be as misleading an illusion as ever was dangled before the eyes of poor humanity. And there have been many of them.

That which lies before the human race is a constant struggle to maintain and improve, in opposition to the State of Nature, the State of Art of an organized polity; in which, and by which, man may develop a worthy civilization, capable of maintaining and constantly improving itself, until the evolution of our globe shall have entered so far upon its downward course that the cosmic process resumes its sway; and, once more, the State of Nature prevails over the surface of our planet.

PART FIVE

Progress Denied

1 Jacob Burckhardt

Despite the fashionableness of the ideas of progress and evolution in the nineteenth century, it was also the age of "historicism," the view that history is an autonomous discipline and that historical events must be studied in their own terms, since they are all equally "immediate to God." The attempt to force history into a pattern dictated by the premises of science or philosophy or religion was rejected by many historians as wholly illegitimate. At first the historicist attitude had little effect on thought outside the ranks of professional historians. Hegel, Comte, Marx, Darwin, and Spencer were the men of the hour, and they all explained away the complexity of history by means of formulas derived from extrahistorical thought and research. But in the last few decades before 1914, historicism began to invade philosophy itself, through the work of such philosophically minded historians as Jacob Burckhardt and such historically minded philosophers as Wilhelm Dilthey and Benedetto Croce. The relativistic implications of historicism are quite clear: if historical events can be understood only in terms of their historical context, in terms of the life and spirit of the age, then historians have no criteria by which to define progress. Each age has its own particular quality, but it becomes illegitimate to import extrahistorical criteria into the study of history in order to be able to rank ages according to some universal scale or schema of values. The possibility of tracing the "progress" of mankind in historical time vanishes.

One of the first historicists to disavow progress was the Swiss historian Jacob Burckhardt (1818-1897), best known today as the author of The Civilization of the Renaissance in Italy. *In that book, Burckhardt may appear to be glorifying modern man, but his thoughts on the historical process as a whole led in a very different direction. The passage reprinted below comes from a lecture, "On Fortune and*

SOURCE. From *Force and Freedom: Reflections on History*, by Jacob Burckhardt, Mary D. Hottinger, translator, and James Hastings Nichols, editor, 1943, New York: Pantheon Books, Inc., pp. 351–363. Copyright 1943 by Pantheon Books, Inc., a division of Random House, Inc. Reprinted by permission of Random House, Inc.

Misfortune in History," given in Basel in 1871, but not published until
after his death.

By an optical illusion, we see happiness at certain times, in certain countries, and we deck it out with analogies from the youth
of man, spring, sunrise and other metaphors. Indeed, we imagine
it dwelling in a beautiful part of the country, a certain house, just
as the smoke rising from a distant cottage in the evening gives us
the impression of intimacy among those living there.

Whole epochs, too, are regarded as happy or unhappy. The
happy ones are the so-called high epochs of man. For instance,
the claim to such happiness is seriously put forward for the
Periclean Age, in which it is recognized that the life of the
ancient world reached its zenith in the State, society, art and
poetry. Other epochs of the same kind, e.g. the age of the good
Emperors, have been abandoned as having been selected from too
one-sided a standpoint. Yet even Renan[1] says of the thirty years
from 1815 to 1848 that they were the best that France, and perhaps humanity, had ever experienced.

All times of great destruction naturally count as eminently
unhappy, since the happiness of the victor is (quite rightly) left
out of account.

Judgments of this kind are characteristic of modern times and
only imaginable with modern historical methods. The ancient
world believed in an original golden age, with respect to which
the world had steadily deteriorated. Hesiod paints the "present"
age of iron in sinister tints of night. In our day, we may note a
theory of perfection (so-called progress) in favor of the present
and the future. Discoveries in pre-history reveal at least this
much—that the pre-historical epochs of the human race were
probably spent in profound torpor, half-animal fear, cannibalism,
etc. In any case, those epochs which have hitherto been regarded
as the youth of the individual peoples, namely those in which
they can first be recognized, were actually very derivative and
late epochs.

[1] *Questions Contemporaines*, p. 44.

But who is, as a rule, responsible for such judgments?

They arise from a kind of literary consensus which has gradually taken shape out of the desires and arguments of the Age of Reason and the real or imagined conclusions of a number of widely read historians.

Nor do they spread haphazard. They are turned to journalistic uses as arguments for or against certain trends of the time. They form part of the fussy baggage of public opinion and, in part, bear very clearly in the very violence, not to say crudity, of their appearance, the impress of the time from which they issue. They are the deadly enemies of true historical insight.

And now we may enquire into some of their separate sources.

The most important of these is *impatience*, and it is the writer and the reader of history who are most subject to it. It supervenes when we have had to spend too long a time on a period, and the evidence—or perhaps our own effort—is inadequate to enable us to form an opinion. We wish things had moved more quickly, and would, for instance, willingly sacrifice one or two of the twenty-six dynasties of Egypt if only King Amasis and his liberal reform would at last carry the day. The Kings of Media, though only four in number, make us impatient because we know so little about them, while that great mover of the imagination, Cyrus, seems to be already waiting at the door.

In short, we take sides for what our ignorance finds interesting against the tedious, as if for happiness against unhappiness. We confuse what was desirable to remote epochs (if anything was) with the pleasures of our imagination.

From time to time we try to delude ourselves with an apparently nobler explanation, but our only motive is one of retrospective impatience.

We pity for their unhappiness past ages, peoples, parties, creeds and so on which passed through long struggles for a higher good. Today we should like to see the aims with which we sympathize triumph without a struggle, and pluck victory without effort; and we transfer the same wish to the past. We pity, for instance, the Roman plebeians and the pre-Solonian Athenians in their century-long struggle with the hard-hearted patricians and Eupatridae and the pitiless debtors' law.

Yet it was only the long struggle which made victory possible and proved the vitality and great worth of the cause.

But how short-lived was the triumph, and how ready we are to side with one decadence against another! Through the victory of democracy, Athens declined into political impotence; Rome conquered Italy, and ultimately the world, at the cost of infinite suffering to the nations and great degeneration at home.

The state of mind which would like to spare the past its troubles, however, comes out most strongly in connection with the wars of religion. We are indignant that any truth (or what we regard as such) should have only been able to make headway by material force, and that it should be suppressed if that force proved inadequate. And it is true that truth infallibly sacrifices something of its purity and sanctity during prolonged struggles, owing to the worldly intentions of its representatives and devotees. Thus it seems to us a misfortune that the Reformation had to contend with a terrible material opposition and hence had to be represented by governments whose heart was in the property of the Church rather than in religion.

Yet in struggle, and in struggle alone, and not in printed polemics, does the full, complete life develop that must come of religious warfare. Only struggle makes both sides fully conscious. Only through struggle, at all times and in all questions of world history, does mankind realize what it really wants and what it can really achieve.

Firstly, Catholicism again became a religion, which it had almost ceased to be. Then men's minds were opened in a thousand directions, political life and culture were brought into all kinds of contact and contrast with the religious conflict, and ultimately the world was transformed and spiritually vastly enriched. None of these things could have come about in mere smooth obedience to the new creed.

Then comes the judgment according to *Culture*. It consists in appraising the felicity and morality of a people or a state of life in the past by the diffusion of education, of general culture and comfort in the modern sense. Here nothing stands the test and all past ages are disposed of with more or less commiseration. For a time, the "present" was literally synonymous with progress, and the result was the most ridiculous vanity, as if the world were marching towards a perfection of mind or even morality. Imperceptibly, the criterion of security, which will be discussed later, creeps in, and without security, and without the culture just described, *we*, at any rate, could not live. But a simple, strong mode of life, with the physical nobility of the race still intact, and the people perpetually on its guard against enemies and oppressors, is also culture, and possibly productive of a superior quality of feeling. Man's mind was complete early in time. And the enquiry as to "moral progress" we may justifiably leave to Buckle, who was so naïvely astonished that there is none to be found, forgetting that it is relevant to the life of the individual and not to whole epochs. If, even in bygone times, men gave their lives for each other, we have not progressed since.

Now follows the judgment by *personal taste*, under which we may group a number of factors. It regards such times and peoples as happy in and among whom precisely that element was predominant which lies nearest the heart of whoever is passing judgment. According as feeling, imagination or reason is the central value of life, the palm will go to those times and peoples in which the largest possible number of men were seriously occupied with spiritual things, or in which art and poetry were the reigning powers, and the greatest possible amount of time was free for intellectual work and contemplation, or in which the greatest number of people could earn a good livelihood and there was unimpeded activity in trade and traffic.

It would be easy to make the representatives of all these three categories realize how one-sided is their judgment, how inadequately it comprehends the whole life of the age concerned, and how intolerable, for many reasons, they themselves would have found life in that age.

Judgment by *political sympathy* is also common. To one, only republics were happy; to another, only monarchies. To one, only times of great and incessant unrest; to another, only times of calm. We might here quote Gibbon's view of the age of the good Emperors as the happiest the human race had ever lived through.

Even in the cases already mentioned, and more especially in the case of judgment by *culture*, the criterion of *security* creeps in. According to this judgment, the prime condition of any happiness is the subordination of private purposes to a police-protected law, the treatment of all questions of property by an impartial legal code and the most far-reaching safeguarding of profits and commerce. The whole morality of our day is to a large extent oriented towards this security, that is, the individual is relieved of the most vital decisions in the defence of house and home, in the majority of cases at any rate. And what goes beyond the power of the State is taken over by insurance, i.e. the forestalling of definite kinds of misfortune by a corresponding annual sacrifice. As soon as a livelihood or its revenues has become sufficiently valuable, the neglect to insure it is considered culpable.

Now this security was grievously lacking at many times which otherwise shine with an immortal radiance and till the end of time will hold a high place in the history of man.

Piracy was of everyday occurrence, not only in the age which Homer describes, but obviously in that in which he lived, and strangers were quite courteously and ingenuously questioned on the subject. The world was swarming with murderers, voluntary and involuntary, who sat at kings' tables, and even Odysseus, in one of his fictitious stories of his life, lays claim to a murder. And yet what simplicity and nobility of manners those people knew! And an age in which the epic lay was the common property of many singers, and moved from place to place, the common delight of nations, is for ever enviable for its achievements, its emotions, its strength and its simplicity. We have only to think of the figure of Nausicaa.

The Periclean Age in Athens was in every sense of the word an age in which any peaceful and prudent citizen of our time would refuse to live, in which he could not but be mortally unhappy, even if he was neither a member of the slave-majority nor a citizen of a city under the Attic hegemony, but a free man and a full citizen of Athens itself. Huge contributions levied by the State, and perpetual inquisitions into the fulfilment of duties towards the State by demagogues and sycophants, were the order of the day. Yet the Athenians of that age must have felt a plenitude of life which far outweighed any security in the world.

A very popular judgment in our day is the judgment by *greatness*. Those who pass such judgment cannot, of course, deny that great political power rapidly acquired, whether by the State or by the individual, can only be bought at the cost of untold sufferings to others. But they ennoble the character of the ruler and those about him to the utmost limit, and attribute to him the prophetic vision of all the great and good results which later came of his work. Finally, they assume that the spectacle of genius must have transfigured and made happy the people he had to deal with.

They dismiss the sufferings of the multitude with the utmost coolness as a "temporary misfortune"; they point to the undeniable fact that settled conditions, i.e. subsequent "happiness," have only been established when terrible struggles have bestowed power on one side or the other. As a rule, the origin and life of the man who applies this standard is based on conditions established in that fashion, hence his indulgence.

And now at last the common source trickling through all these judgments, and long since perceptible in them, the judgment by *egoism*. "We" judge thus and thus. It is true that somebody else, who is of the contrary opinion—perhaps out of egoism too—also says "we," while in the absolute sense as much is achieved by both as by the prayers of the individual farmer for sun or rain.

Our profound and utterly ridiculous self-seeking first regards those times as happy which are in some way akin to our nature. Further, it considers such past forces and individuals as praiseworthy on whose work our present existence and relative welfare are based.

Just as if the world and its history had existed merely for our sakes! For everyone regards all times as fulfilled in his own, and cannot see his own as one of many passing waves. If he has reason to believe that he has achieved pretty nearly everything that lay in his power, we can understand his standpoint. If he looks for change, he hopes that he will soon see it come, and may help to bring it about.

But every individual—we too—exists not for his own sake, but for the sake of all the past and all the future.

In face of this great, grave whole, the claims of peoples, times and individuals to happiness and well-being, lasting or fleeting, is of very subordinate importance, for since the life of humanity is one whole, it is only to our frail powers of perception that its fluctuations in time or place are a rise and fall, fortune and misfortune. The truth is that they are governed by a higher necessity.

We should try to rid the life of nations entirely of the word "happiness" and replace it by some other, while, as we shall see later, we cannot do without the word "unhappiness." Natural history shows us a fearful struggle for life, and that same struggle encroaches far upon the historical life of nations.

"Happiness" is a desecrated word, exhausted by common use. Supposing that there was a world plebiscite to decide on the definition of the word. How far should we get?

And above all, only the fairy-tale equates changelessness with happiness. From its childish standpoint it may strive to hold fast to the image of a permanent, joyous well-being (about half-way between Olympus and the Land of Cockayne). But even the fairy-tale does not take it really seriously. When the wicked magician at last lies dead and the wicked fairies are punished, Abdullah and Fatima live happily ever after into a ripe old age, but imagination, their trials over, forthwith dismisses them, to claim our interest for Hassan and Zuleika or Leila, or some other couple. The end of the *Odyssey* is so much nearer the truth. The trials of him who has suffered so much are to continue, and he must at once set out on a grievous pilgrimage.

The conception of a happiness which consists in the permanence of certain conditions is of its very nature false. The moment we set aside a primitive state, or state of nature, in which every day is like every other day, and every century like every other century, until, by some rupture, historical life begins, we must admit that permanence means paralysis and death. Only in movement, with all its pain, is life. And above all, the idea of happiness as a positive feeling is false in itself. Happiness is mere absence of pain, at best associated with a faint sense of growth.

There have been, of course, arrested peoples who present the same general picture for centuries and hence give the impression of tolerable contentment with their fate. As a rule, however, that is the product of despotism, which inevitably appears when a form of State and society has been achieved (presumably at great cost) and has to be defended against the rise of opposing forces, and with all available measures, even the most extreme. The first generation must, as a rule, have been very unhappy, but succeeding ones grow up in that order of ideas, and ultimately they pronounce sacred everything that they cannot and do not wish to change, praising it perhaps as supreme happiness. When Spain was on the point of material extinction, she was still capable of deep feeling as soon as the splendor of the Castilian name came into question. The oppression of the government and the Inquisition seems to have been powerless to humiliate her soul. Her greatest artists and poets belong to that age.

These stationary peoples and national epochs may exist in order to preserve definite spiritual, intellectual and material values from earlier times and to pass them on uncontaminated as a leaven to the future. And their calm is not absolute and deathly; it is rather of the nature of a refreshing sleep.

There are other ages, peoples, men, on the other hand, which at times spend their strength, indeed their whole strength, in rapid movement. Their importance resides in the destruction of the old and the clearing of the way for the new. But they were not made for any lasting happiness, or indeed for any passing joy, save for the short-lived rejoicing of victory. For their power of regeneration is born of perpetual discontent, which finds any halt tedious and demands to advance.

Now this striving, however important its consequences, however great its political consequences may be, actually appears in time in the garb of the most unfathomable human egoism, which must of necessity subdue others to its will and find its satisfaction in their obedience, yet which is insatiable in its thirst for obedience and admiration and claims the right to use force in all great issues.

Now evil on earth is assuredly a part of the great economy of world history. It is force, the right of the stronger over the weaker, prefigured in that struggle for life which fills all nature, the animal and the vegetable worlds, and is carried on in the early stages of humanity by murder and robbery, by the eviction, extermination or enslavement of weaker races, or of weaker peoples within the same race, of weaker States, of weaker social classes within the same State and people.[2]

Yet the stronger, as such, is far from being the better. Even in the vegetable kingdom, we can see baser and bolder species making headway here and there. In history, however, the defeat of the noble simply because it is in the minority is a grave danger, especially in times ruled by a very general culture which arrogates to itself the rights of the majority. The forces which have succumbed were perhaps nobler and better, but the victorious, though their only motive was ambition, inaugurate a future of which they themselves have no inkling. Only in the exemption of States from the general moral law, which continues to be binding on the individual, can something like a premonition of it be divined.

The greatest example is offered by the Roman Empire, inaugurated by the most frightful methods soon after the end of the struggle between the patricians and plebeians in the guise of the Samnite War, and completed by the subjection of East and West in rivers of blood.

Here, on the grand scale, we can discern a historical purpose which is, to us at any rate, plainly apparent, namely the creation of a common world culture, which also made possible the spread of a world religion, both capable of being transmitted to the Teutonic barbarians of the Völkerwanderung [migrations] as the future bond of a new Europe.

Yet from the fact that good came of evil, and relative happiness

---

[2] Cf. Hartmann's prophecy. *Philosophie des Unbewussten*, pp. 341–3: English transl. *The Philosophy of the Unconscious*, Vol. II, Ch. X. pp. 11–13.

of misery, we cannot in any way deduce that evil and misery were not, at the outset, what they were. Every successful act of violence is evil, and at the very least a dangerous example. But when that act was the foundation of power, it was followed by the indefatigable efforts of men to turn mere power into law and order. With their healthy strength, they set to work to cure the State of violence.

And, at times, evil reigns long as evil on earth, and not only among Fatimids and Assassins. According to Christian doctrine, the prince of this world is Satan. There is nothing more unchristian than to promise virtue a lasting reign, a material divine reward here below, as the early Church writers did to the Christian Emperors. Yet evil, as ruler, is of supreme importance; it is the one condition of selfless good. It would be a horrible sight if, as a result of the consistent reward of good and punishment of evil on this earth, all men were to behave well with an ulterior motive, for they would continue to be evil men and to nourish evil in their hearts. The time might come when men would pray Heaven for a little impunity for evildoers, simply in order that they might show their real nature once more. There is enough hypocrisy in the world as it is.

2   Reinhold Niebuhr

Since 1914, the idea of progress has been under attack from all quarters. Historicism continues to play its part in this assault, but the chief impetus has come from man's massive disillusionment with himself in the era of total war and the total state. This disillusionment is perhaps best articulated by theological writers, such as the American thinker Reinhold Niebuhr (1892-   ), who can argue that man's dream

SOURCE: Reinhold Niebuhr, *Faith and History: A Comparison of Christian and Modern Views of History*, New York: Scribner's, 1949, pp. 1–12 and 231–234. Copyright 1949 by Charles Scribner's Sons. Reprinted with the permission of Charles Scribner's Sons and the author.

*of progress was a product of modern arrogance, doomed to collapse
under the weight of original sin. Notice that two of our late nineteenth-century writers, Huxley and Burckhardt, also had a great deal
to say about human incorrigibility.*

It would have been difficult for the generations of the twentieth
century to survive the hazards and to face the perplexities of our
age in any event, since every problem of human existence had
been given a wider scope than known in previous ages. But our
perplexities became the more insoluble and the perils to which
we were exposed became the more dangerous because the men of
this generation had to face the rigors of life in the twentieth century with nothing but the soft illusions of the previous two centuries to cover their spiritual nakedness. There was nothing in the
creeds and dogmas of these centuries which would have enabled
modern men either to anticipate or to understand the true nature
of the terrors and tumults to which they would be exposed.

The history of mankind exhibits no more ironic experience than
the contrast between the sanguine hopes of recent centuries and
the bitter experiences of contemporary man. Every technical advance, which previous generations regarded as a harbinger or
guarantor of the redemption of mankind from its various difficulties, has proved to be the cause, or at least the occasion, for
a new dimension of ancient perplexities.

A single article of faith has given diverse forms of modern
culture the unity of a shared belief. Modern men of all shades of
opinion agreed in the belief that historical development is a redemptive process. It was the genuine achievement of modern
historical science to discover that human culture is subject to indeterminate development. Natural science added the discovery that
nature, as well as human culture and institutions, undergoes an
evolutionary process. Thus the static conception of history which
characterized the Middle Ages as well as antiquity was breached.
It would be more accurate to say that the discoveries of the historical and natural sciences gave modern men a final justification
for a new faith which had been developing since the Renaissance.

Joachim of Flores had given the first intimation of it in the late Middle Ages when he transmuted Christian eschatology into the hope of a transfigured world, of a future age of the Holy Spirit, in which the antinomies and ambiguities of man's historic existence would be overcome in history itself.

The Renaissance, which ostensibly restored classical learning, was actually informed by a very unclassical sense of history. It retained, or returned to, the cyclical interpretation of history, as known in the classical age; but historical cycles became spirals of advance in Renaissance historiography. Its passion for a return to old disciplines was submerged by its enthusiasm for man's new and growing powers. This enthusiasm was increased as evidence accumulated that among man's unique gifts belonged the capacity to increase his freedom and power indeterminately. Had not human institutions developed from crude and barbaric beginnings to their present proud estate? The nineteenth century added to this new certainty not only the assurance that nature itself was subject to growth but also the obvious achievements of applied science. The phenomenal technical advances of the century, outstripping the slow conquest of nature of all previous eras, seemed to be the final proof of the validity of modern man's new faith in history. The classical conception of time as a cycle of endless recurrences was finally overcome. Time was no longer a mystery which required explanation. It became the principle of interpretation by which the mystery of life was comprehended. History was no longer an enigma. It became the assurance of man's redemption from his every ill.

The modern age is variously described as an age of science or as an age of reason. Confidence in the power of reason, and particularly in the inductive and empirical strategy of the rational faculty, is indeed a characteristic of our age. But the classical ages also believed in the power and virtue of reason. Modern culture is distinguished by its confidence, both in the growing power of reason and in its capacity, when rightly disciplined, to assure the development of every human power and virtue.

The dominant note in modern culture is not so much confidence in reason as faith in history. The conception of a redemptive history informs the most diverse forms of modern culture.

The rationalist, Leibnitz, shared it with the romanticist, Herder. Kant's critical idealism was not so obviously informed by the new historical sense as the thought of Hegel, who had reinterpreted Platonism to conform to the historical consciousness of modernity; but Kant was as certain as Hegel of a movement of history toward increasing rationality. J. S. Mill's utilitarianism stood in sharp contradiction to Kant's ethics; but Mill agreed with Kant that history was moving toward a universal concord of life with life. The difference between the French Enlightenment's materialism and the idealism of the German Enlightenment made no appreciable difference in the common historical optimism of both. The French physiocrats believed that progress would be assured by the removal of the irrelevancies of historical restraints from the operation of the laws of nature; while Comte thought it would be achieved by bringing social process under the control of an elite of social scientists. But this contrast between determinism and voluntarism (which is, incidentally, never composed in modern culture) had no influence upon the shared belief in progress. There is only a slight difference in optimism between the deterministic thought of Herbert Spencer and the modern voluntarism of John Dewey.

Even Karl Marx, who introduced a provisional historical catastrophism to challenge the optimism of bourgeois life, did not shake the modern conception of a redemptive history basically. He saw in the process of historical development certain "dialectical" elements not observed in bourgeois theories. He knew that there is disintegration as well as increasing integration in history; that there is death as well as growth. But he also believed that a new life and a new age would rise out of the death of an old one with dialectical necessity. Catastrophe was the certain prelude of redemption in his scheme of salvation. The ultimate similarity between Marxist and bourgeois optimism, despite the provisional catastrophism of the former, is, in fact, the most telling proof of the unity of modern culture. It is a unity which transcends warring social philosophies, conflict between which contributed to the refutation of a common hope.

The goal toward which history was presumably moving was variously defined. The most unreflective forms of historical optimism in the nineteenth century assumed that increasing physical comfort and well-being were the guarantee of every other form of advance. Sometimes the enlarging human community was believed to be developing inevitably toward a universal community, for "clans and tribes, long narrowly self-regarding, are finally enlarged and compacted into nations; and nations move inevitably, however slowly, into relations with one another, whose ultimate goal is the unification of mankind."[1] It may be recorded in passing that scarcely a single student in the modern era noted the marked difference between the task of unifying tribes, nations and empires and the final task of the unification of mankind. In the former case there is always some particular force of geography, language, common experience or the fear of a common foe which furnishes the core of cohesion. In the latter case unity must be achieved in defiance of the unique and particularistic forces of historical concretion.

Sometimes, as in H. G. Wells' *Outline of History*, the historical process is assumed to be moving toward the democratization, as well as the universalization, of the human community. The democratic culmination, toward which history was presumably moving was frequently defined in contradictory terms. Libertarians thought they saw a movement toward increasing liberty while equalitarians and collectivists thought they could discern a movement toward more intense social cohesion.

Nor was there agreement about the cause of historical advance. Social Darwinism as well as other forms of naturalism looked upon historical development as a mere extension of natural evolution. The Darwinists saw the guarantee of progress in the survival of the fittest. Others discerned a movement in both nature and history from consistent egoism to a greater and greater consideration of the interests of others.[2]

---

[1] Edmund Noble, *Purposive Evolution*, p. 418.

[2] Prince Kropotkin in *Mutual Aid* traced the development from limited mutual aid in the animal world to wider and wider extensions of mutuality. Leslie Stephen described an evolutionary development of conscience as the "gradual growth of social tissue." (*The Science of Ethics*, p. 120.)

W. K. Clifford equated an evolutionary development of the moral sense with the growth of a "tribal self." (*Lectures and Essays*, II, p. 110.)

More frequently historical development was regarded not so much as an extension of forces operative in nature as a negation of natural impulses through the growth of mind. The method of reason's triumph over the irrationalities of nature was, however, variously interpreted. The French Enlightenment assigned reason the primary function of discerning the "laws of nature" and of destroying man's abortive efforts to circumvent these laws. Comte, on the other hand, believed that a scientific political program would bring the irrational factors in man's common life under rational control. Condorcet believed that justice would triumph when universal education destroyed the advantage which the shrewd had over the simple. Or it was assumed that increasing rationality would gradually destroy the irrational (primarily religious) justifications of special privilege.[3] Or that increasing reason would gradually prompt all men to grant their fellowmen justice, the power of logic requiring that the interests of each individual be brought into a consistent scheme of value.[4] More recently the psychological sciences have hoped for the increasing control or elimination of self-regarding impulses and the extension of human sympathy through the rational control of man's sub-rational life.

Though modern culture is predominantly rationalistic, so that even naturalistic philosophies place their primary confidence in increasing rationality, the subordinate romantic distrust of reason must not be obscured. Romanticism in its most consistent form has a preference for the primitive, which implies a pessimistic estimate of the growth of civilization. Rousseau's dictum that men were born free and are now everywhere in chains led to a provisional pessimism; but this did not prevent him from elaborating a system of historical optimism, based on confidence in the possibility of bringing all competing wills into the concurrence of a general will. Bergson's distrust of reason likewise failed to arrest his optimistic conclusions about historical development. He placed his confi-

---

[3] This is the thesis of Robert Briffault's *Rational Evolution*.

[4] L. T. Hobhouse bases his confidence in progress upon this argument in *Principles of Social Justice, The Rational Good,* and *Development and Purpose.*

dence in the growth of a mystical capacity, which would lift men from particular to universal loyalties.[5]

The fact that the prevailing mood of modern culture was able to transmute the original pessimism of romanticism into an optimistic creed proves the power of this mood. Only occasionally the original pessimism erupts in full vigor, as in the thought of a Schopenhauer or Nietzsche. The subjugation of romantic pessimism, together with the transmutation of Marxist catastrophism establishes historical optimism far beyond the confines of modern rationalism. Though there are minor dissonances the whole chorus of modern culture learned to sing the new song of hope in remarkable harmony. The redemption of mankind, by whatever means, was assured for the future. It was, in fact, assured by the future.

II

There were experiences in previous centuries which might well have challenged this unqualified optimism. But the expansion of man's power over nature proceeded at such a pace that all doubts were quieted, allowing the nineteenth century to become the "century of hope"[6] and to express the modern mood in its most extravagant terms. History, refusing to move by the calendar, actually permitted the nineteenth century to indulge its illusions into the twentieth. Then came the deluge. Since 1914 one tragic experience has followed another, as if history had been designed to refute the vain delusions of modern man.

The "laws" and tendencies of historical development proved in the light of contemporary experience to be much more complex than any one had supposed. Every new freedom represented a new peril as well as a new promise. Modern industrial society dissolved ancient forms of political authoritarianism; but the tyrannies which grew on its soil proved more brutal and vexatious than the old ones. The inequalities rooted in landed property were levelled. But the more dynamic inequalities of a technical society became more perilous to the community than the more static forms

---

[5] *Cf.* Henri Bergson, *Two Sources of Religion and Morality.*
[6] *Cf.* F. S. Marvin, *The Century of Hope.*

of uneven power. The achievement of individual liberty was one of the genuine advances of bourgeois society. But this society also created atomic individuals who, freed from the disciplines of the older organic communities, were lost in the mass; and became the prey of demagogues and charlatans who transmuted their individual anxieties and resentments into collective political power of demonic fury.

The development of instruments of communication and transportation did create a potential world community by destroying all the old barriers of time and space. But the new interdependence of the nations created a more perplexing problem than anyone had anticipated. It certainly did not prompt the nations forthwith to organize a "parliament of man and federation of the world." Rather it extended the scope of old international frictions so that a single generation was subjected to two wars of global dimensions. Furthermore the second conflict left the world as far from the goal of global peace as the first. At its conclusion the world's peace was at the mercy of two competing alliances of world savers, the one informed by the bourgeois and the other by the proletarian creed of world redemption. Thus the civil war in the heart of modern industrial nations, which had already brought so much social confusion into the modern world, was re-enacted in the strife between nations. The development of atomic instruments of conflict aggravated the fears not only of those who lacked such instruments, but of those who had them. The fears of the latter added a final ironic touch to the whole destiny of modern man. The possession of power has never annulled the fears of those who wield it, since it prompts them to anxiety over its possible loss. The possession of a phenomenal form of destructive power in the modern day has proved to be so fruitful of new fears that the perennial ambiguity of man's situation of power and weakness became more vividly exemplified, rather than overcome. Thus a century which was meant to achieve a democratic society of world-scope finds itself at its half-way mark uncertain about the possibility of avoiding a new conflict of such proportions as to leave the survival of mankind, or at least the survival of civilization, in doubt.

The tragic irony of this refutation by contemporary history of modern man's conception of history embodies the spiritual crisis of our age. Other civilizations have assumed their own indestructibility, usually indulging in pretensions of immortality in a "golden age," precisely when their ripeness was turning into over-ripeness and portents of their disintegration were becoming discernible. It remained for the culture of the Renaissance and Enlightenment to raise this *Hybris* of civilizations to a new and absurd height by claiming to have found the way of arresting the decay not merely of a particular civilization but of civilization as such. Was not the "scientific conquest of nature" a "sure method" by which the "wholesale permanent decay of civilization has become impossible"?[7] Had not the scientific method established the dominion of man over nature in place of "the dominion of man over the labor of others" which was the "shaky basis" of older civilizations?

Contemporary experience represents a *Nemesis* which is justly proportioned in its swiftness and enormity to the degree of *Hybris* which had expressed itself in modern life. In one century modern man had claimed to have achieved the dizzy heights of the mastery both of natural process and historical destiny. In the following century he is hopelessly enmeshed in an historical fate, threatening mutual destruction, from which he seems incapable of extricating himself. A word of Scripture fits the situation perfectly: "He that sitteth in the heavens shall laugh: the Lord shall have them in derision" (Psalms 2:4).

The modern experience belongs in the category of pathos or irony rather than tragedy, because contemporary culture has no vantage point of faith from which to understand the predicament of modern man. It is therefore incapable either of rising to a tragic defiance of destiny, as depicted in Greek drama, or of achieving a renewal of life through a contrite submission to destiny, as in Christian tragedy. Subsequent centuries (if, indeed, there be survivors capable of reflecting upon the meaning of the experience of this age) may discern in it the pathos characteristic of Thomas Hardy's novels. For the actors in the drama are enmeshed in an inscrutable fate, which either drives them to despair or for which

[7] John Dewey, in *International Journal of Ethics*, April 1916, p. 313.

they find false interpretations.

Most of the explanations of contemporary catastrophe are derived from principles of interpretation which were responsible for modern man's inability to anticipate the experiences which he now seeks to comprehend. A culture, rooted in historical optimism, naturally turns first of all to the concepts of "retrogression" and "reversion" to explain its present experience. Thus Nazism is interpreted as a "reversion to barbarism" or even as a "reversion to the cruelty of the Middle Ages." We are assured that mankind has no right to expect an uninterrupted ascent toward happiness and perfection. Comfort is drawn from the figure of a "spiral" development. This is usually accompanied by the assurance that no recession ever reaches the depth of previous ones and that each new "peak" achieves a height beyond those of the past. This spiral version of the concept of progress is hardly more adequate than the simpler version; for both the failures and achievements of advanced civilizations are incommensurable with those of simpler societies. To call them better or worse by comparison is almost meaningless. Insofar as comparisons can be made it is idle to regard the tyrannies and anarchies which result from the breakdown of an advanced and highly integrated civilization as preferable to the social confusion of more primitive societies.

An equally favored mode of reassurance is to take a long view of history, to enlarge upon the millennia of pre-historic barbarism which preceded the known, and comparatively brief, period of civilized life, and to express the hope that present misfortunes belong to the period of civilization's infancy which will be forgotten in the unimagined heights of perfection which will be achieved in the unimagined subsequent ages. So James Bryce wrote in the period of disillusionment, following the first world war: "Shaken out of that confident hope in progress . . . mankind must resume its efforts toward improvement in a chastened mood, . . . consoled by the reflection that it has taken a thousand years to emerge from savagery and less than half that time to rise above the shameless sensualities of the ancient world and the ruthless ferocity of the Dark Ages."[8]

[8] *Modern Democracies*, Vol. II, p. 607 (1921).

A modern biologist seeks comfort in a similar logic: "When world wide wars, with their indescribable sufferings and horrors, brutalities and tyrannies shake one's faith in human progress, it is comforting to take a long view of cosmic evolution and remember that the longest wars are but a fraction of a second on the clock of life on earth, and that 'eternal process moving on' is not likely to stop today or tomorrow."[9]

These comforting assurances rest upon the dubious assumption that the "shameless sensualities" of the ancient world and the "ruthless ferocity" of the Dark Ages have no counterpart in modern life. The belief that human brutality is a vestigial remnant of man's animal or primitive past represents one of the dearest illusions of modern culture, to which men cling tenaciously even when every contemporary experience refutes it.

The appeal to future millennia of the world's history, in comparison with which past history is but a brief episode and its periods of conflict but seconds on the clock of time, is hardly reassuring when for instance the history of warfare in this brief episode is considered. For that history contains the development from partial and limited to total wars; and the evolution of means of combat from spears to atomic bombs. To be sure historical developments as progress in the lethal efficacy of our means of means of destruction. But the fact that history contains such developments as progress in the lethal efficacy of our means of destruction and the increasing consistency of tyrannical governments must prove the vanity of our hope in historical development as such. The prospect of the extension of history into untold millennia must, if these facts are considered, sharpen, rather than assuage, man's anxiety about himself and his history.

A more favored explanation of present catastrophes is to hold the "cultural lag" responsible for them, which means to attribute them to the failure of man's social wisdom to keep pace with his technical advances. This explanation has the merit of being quite true as an interpretation of specific evils, arising from specific maladjustments between a culture and its social institutions, or between the economic and technical arrangements of an era and its

---

[9] Edward G. Conklin, *Man: Real and Ideal*, pp. 205–206.

political forms. It nevertheless hides a profound illusion with reference to the total situation.

One of the most potent causes of historical evil is the inability of men to bring their customs and institutions into conformity with new situations. Political institutions developed in a pastoral society maintain themselves stubbornly in an agrarian economy; and agrarian institutions are projected into a commercial age. In a period of rapid technical advance these maladjustments are a source of great social confusion. It is obvious, for instance, that the sometimes extravagant individualism of the commercial age is not an adequate social philosophy for the intense social cohesion of a new industrial age; and that the national sovereignties of the past must be abridged to permit the growth of international political institutions, consonant with the economic interdependence of modern nations. All this is clear.

The error embodied in the theory of the cultural lag is the modern assumption that the "cultural lag" is due merely to the tardiness of the social sciences in achieving the same standards of objectivity and disinterestedness which characterize the natural sciences. This belief embodies the erroneous idea that man's knowledge and conquest of nature develops the wisdom and the technics required for the knowledge and the conquest of human nature.

It is man in the unity of his being who must come to terms with his fellowmen and, for that matter, with himself. Scientific knowledge of what human nature is and how it reacts to various given social situations will always be of service in refashioning human conduct. But ultimately the problems of human conduct and social relations are in a different category from the relations of physical nature. The ability to judge friend or foe with some degree of objectivity is, in the ultimate instance, a moral and not an intellectual achievement, since it requires the mitigation of fears and prejudices, envies and hatreds which represent defects, not of the mind, but of the total personality. Moreover, the ability to yield to the common good, to forgo special advantages for a larger measure of social justice, to heal the breach between warring factions by forgiveness, or to acknowledge a common human predicament between disputants in a social situation, is the fruit of a social wisdom to which science makes only ancillary contributions. This type of wisdom involves the whole of man in the unity of his being. The modern belief that "scientific objectivity" may be simply extended from the field of nature to the field of history obscures the unity of the self which acts, and is acted upon, in history. It also obscures the ambiguity of the human self; for the self as the creature of history is the same self which must be the creator of history. The creaturely limitations which corrupt his actions as creator are, however, never the limitations of mere ignorance. The self as creator does not master the self as creature merely by the extension of scientific technics. The hope that everything recalcitrant in human behaviour may be brought under the subjection of the inclusive purposes of "mind" by the same technics which gained man mastery over nature is not merely an incidental illusion, prompted by the phenomenal achievements of the natural sciences. It is the culminating error in modern man's misunderstanding of himself. Thus the principle of comprehension by which modern culture seeks to understand our present failure belongs to the misunderstanding about man's life and history which contributed to that failure. The spiritual confusions arising from this misunderstanding constitute the cultural crisis of our age, beyond and above the political crisis in which our civilization is involved.

The contradiction between the hopes of yesterday and the realities of today has created something like despair in those parts of the world where past stabilities have been most seriously shaken; and it is generating a kind of desperate complacency in those parts of the world in which the crisis of the age is dimly, though not fully, sensed.

The time is ripe, at any rate, to survey both the modern and the Christian and classical ideas of man's relation to history. Such a study may reveal the roots of modern misconceptions about man's history more clearly and it may restore the relevance of previous answers to the problem of human destiny, which were prematurely discarded.

*   *   *

The knowledge that "the world passeth away and the lusts thereof" and that every *civitas terrena* [earthly city] is a city of destruction does not, however, negate the permanent values which appear in the rise and fall of civilizations and cultures. A feudal civilization may be destroyed by its inability to incorporate the new dynamism of a commercial and industrial society. But there are qualities of organic community, including even the hierarchial organization of the community, in a feudal society, which transcend the fate of such a civilization. In the same manner a bourgeois society, though involved in a self-destructive individualism, also contributes to the emancipation of the individual in terms of permanent worth. There are thus facets of the eternal in the flux of time. From the standpoint of Biblical faith the eternal in the temporal flux is not so much a permanent structure of existence, revealed in the cycle of change, as it is a facet of the *Agape* of Christ. It is "love which abideth." An organic society may achieve a harmony of life with life without freedom. Insofar as it is without freedom it is not a perfect incarnation of *Agape*. But insofar as it is a harmony of life with life it is an imperfect symbol of the true *Agape*. A libertarian society may sacrifice community to the dignity of the individual. But insofar as it emancipates the individual from social restraints which are less than the restraints of love, it illustrates another facet of the full dimension of *Agape*. Thus the same civilizations which perish because they violate the law of love at some point may also contribute a deathless value insofar as they explicate the harmony of life with life intended in creation.

If this be so, the question arises why the process of history should not gradually gather up the timeless values and eliminate the worthless. Why should not history be a winnowing process in which truth is separated from falsehood; and the falsehood burned as chaff, while the wheat of truth is "gathered into the barn." In that case *die Weltgeschichte* [world history] would, after all, be *das Weltgericht* [the world tribunal]. There is one sense in which this is true. Yet this conception of history as its own judge is finally false. It is true in the sense that history is actually the story of man's developing freedom. Insofar as increasing freedom leads to harmonies of life with life within communities and between communities, in which the restraints and cohesions of nature are less determinative for the harmony than the initiative of men, a positive meaning must be assigned to growth in history. There is, certainly, positive significance in the fact that modern man must establish community in global terms or run the risk of having his community destroyed even on the level of the local village. To establish community in global terms requires the exercise of the ingenuity of freedom far beyond the responsibilities of men of other epochs, who had the support of natural forces, such as consanguinity, for their limited communities. The expansion of the perennial task of achieving a tolerable harmony of life with life under ever higher conditions of freedom and in ever wider frames of harmony represents the residual truth in modern progressive interpretations of history.

But this truth is transmuted into error very quickly if it is assumed that increasing freedom assures the achievement of the wider task. The perils of freedom rise with its promises, and the perils and promises are inextricably interwoven. The parable of the wheat and the tares expresses the Biblical attitude toward the possibilities of history exactly. The servants who desire to uproot the tares which have been sown among the wheat are forbidden to do so by the householder "lest while ye gather up the tares, ye root up also the wheat with them. Let both grow together until the harvest: and in the time of harvest I will say unto the reapers, Gather ye together first the tares, and bind them in bundles to burn them: but gather the wheat into my barn" (Matthew 13: 29–30).

There is, in other words, no possibility of a final judgement within history but only at the end of history. The increase of human freedom over nature is like the advancing season which ripens both wheat and tares, which are inextricably intermingled. This simple symbol from the sayings of our Lord in the synoptics is supplemented in the eschatology of the Epistles, where it is Christ himself who becomes the judge at the final judgement of the world.

History, in short, does not solve the enigma of history. There are facets of meaning in it which transcend the flux of time. These give glimpses of the eternal love which bears the whole project of history. There is a positive meaning also in the ripening of love under conditions of increasing freedom; but the possibility that the same freedom may increase the power and destructiveness of self-love makes it impossible to find a solution for the meaning of history within history itself. Faith awaits a final judgement and a final resurrection. Thus mystery stands at the end, as well as at the beginning of the whole pilgrimage of man. But the clue to the mystery is the *Agape* of Christ. It is the clue to the mystery of Creation. "All things were made by him; and without him was not any thing made that was made" (John 1:3). It is the clue to the mystery of the renewals and redemptions within history, since wherever the divine mercy is discerned as within and above the wrath, which destroys all forms of self-seeking, life may be renewed, individually and collectively. It is also the clue to the final redemption of history. The antinomies of good and evil increase rather than diminish in the long course of history. Whatever provisional meanings there may be in such a process, it must drive men to despair when viewed ultimately, unless they have discerned the power and the mercy which overcomes the enigma of its end.

The whole history of man is thus comparable to his individual life. He does not have the power and the wisdom to overcome the ambiguity of his existence. He must and does increase his freedom, both as an individual and in the total human enterprise; and his creativity is enhanced by the growth of his freedom. But this freedom also tempts him to deny his mortality and the growth of freedom and power increases the temptation. But evils in history are the consequence of this pretension. Confusion follows upon man's effort to complete his life by his own power and solve its enigma by his own wisdom. Perplexities, too simply solved, produce despair. The Christian faith is the apprehension of the divine love and power which bears the whole human pilgrimage, shines through its enigmas and antinomies and is finally and definitively revealed in a drama in which suffering love gains triumph over sin and death. This revelation does not resolve all perplexities; but it does triumph over despair, and leads to the renewal of life from self-love to love.

Man, in both his individual life and in his total enterprise, moves from a limited to a more extensive expression of freedom over nature. If he assumes that such an extension of freedom insures and increases emancipation from the bondage of self, he increases the bondage by that illusion. Insofar as the phenomenal increase in human power in a technical age has created that illusion, it has also involved our culture in the profound pathos of disappointed hopes, caused by false estimates of the glory and the misery of man.

To understand, from the standpoint of the Christian faith, that man can not complete his own life, and can neither define nor fulfill the final mystery and meaning of his historical pilgrimage, is not to rob life of meaning or responsibility.

The love toward God and the neighbor, which is the final virtue of the Christian life, is rooted in an humble recognition of the fragmentary character of our own wisdom, virtue and power. The forgiveness which is the most perfect expression of that love, is prompted by a contrite recognition of the guilt with which our own virtue is tainted. Our faith in the faithfulness of God, and our hope in His triumph over the tragic antinomies of life do not annul, but rather transfigure, human wisdom. For they mark the limit of its power and purge it of its pretenses. For "God hath chosen the foolish things of the world to confound the wise; and God hath chosen the weak things of the world to confound the things that are mighty . . . that no flesh should glory in His presence."

3   *Georg G. Iggers*

This article from The American Historical Review *by the intellectual historian Georg G. Iggers (1926-) discusses both of the sources for the disavowal of progress illustrated by the last two selections: historicism, on the one hand, and cultural pessimism and disillusionment with man, on the other. Iggers makes an interesting distinction between the historicism of the earlier nineteenth century, which he labels "historism," and that which follows, "historicism" proper. Both opposed the idea of progress, he argues, but the former retained a fundamental optimism about man, whereas the latter has tended to be pessimistic, relativistic, and disenchanted. In the final pages of the article, Iggers ventures some thoughts of his own on the validity of ideas of progress.*

In the course of the nineteenth century a profound crisis in Western consciousness occurred, perhaps the deepest since the emergence of the great traditional value systems in Greece and Palestine two and a half millenniums ago. The fundamental metaphysical assumption of the Western intellectual tradition, the certainty of the ethical meaningfulness of the universe, collapsed. The full realization of the "death of God," proclaimed by Heinrich Heine, Friedrich Nietzsche, and others, suddenly took hold of Western thought. Modern man confronted what Jean-Paul Sartre has pictured as the logical consequence of the atheistic position,[1] the recognition that he lived in a world without objective

[1] See Jean-Paul Sartre, *Existentialism,* tr. Bernard Frechtman (New York, 1947); see also Heinrich Heine, "Zur Geschichte der Religion und Philosophie in Deutschland," in *Heinrich Heine's Gesammelte Werke,* ed. Gustav Karpeles (2d ed., 9 vols., Berlin, 1893), V, 94.

SOURCE. Georg G. Iggers, "The Idea of Progress: A Critical Reassessment," in *American Historical Review,* LXXI (October, 1965), pp. 1–17. Copyright 1965 by Georg G. Iggers. Reprinted by permission of the author.

value and hence without objective meaning.

In a sense this ethical nihilism was the end product of a long process of secularization of life and thought that had begun in the Middle Ages. The scientific discoveries and formulations of the seventeenth century had ushered in a demythologization of world views. The Enlightenment marked the height of the belief in the applicability of empirical analysis to the problems of human behavior as well as of ethics. Yet, in another way, the gulf which separated the naturalistic world view of the eighteenth-century Enlightenment from the modern denial of the existence of objective value was much deeper than that which separated the demythologized world of the Enlightenment from the religious world picture of the prescientific age. Carl Becker has with justice noted that in a very basic way "the *Philosophes* were nearer the Middle Ages, less emancipated from the preconceptions of medieval Christian thought, than they quite realized or we have commonly supposed."[2] For in their belief that there was a basic moral structure inherent in the universe, the eighteenth-century advocates of natural law still stood in a line of thought that linked them with Isaiah, Aristotle, and Thomas Aquinas.

The relation between the doctrine of natural law and the idea of progress is a complex one. The belief in rational ethical values does not necessarily carry with it the belief in the perfectibility of man. Eighteenth-century rationalist thought was marked by strong undercurrents of pessimism.[3] The doctrine of natural law did not imply that men would act rationally, but merely that they had a rational choice. Voltaire saw in history the perennial struggle of reason and unreason. Nevertheless, without the belief in the existence of rational values, the idea of progress is meaningless. The idea of progress in its classical form was born in the confidence of the Enlightenment that through the systematic application of reason to society, rational conditions of human life could be created. Certain critics, such as Karl Löwith,[4] have therefore

[2] Carl L. Becker, *The Heavenly City of the Eighteenth-Century Philosophers* (New Haven, Conn., 1932), 29.

[3] See Henry Vyverberg, *Historical Pessimism in the French Enlightenment* (Cambridge, Mass., 1958).

[4] See Karl Löwith, *Meaning in History: The Theological Implications of the Philosophy of History* (Chicago, 1949).

interpreted the idea of progress as a secularized form of the Judaeo-Christian conception of Providence. This is true only to the extent that the theorists of progress of the eighteenth and nineteenth centuries viewed history as a unilinear process toward a meaningful end. But not only did most theorists of progress see the fulfillment of this end in worldly terms, but, as in the case of Condorcet and John Stuart Mill (in sharp contrast to the Augustinian view), they emphasized the active role that men played in the historical process through the application of reason and science to society.

What constitutes reason and science, of course, underwent considerable development in the course of the seventeenth and eighteenth centuries. Ernst Cassirer has sharply contrasted pre- and post-Newtonian conceptions of philosophy and science. If most seventeenth-century thinkers still believed that an understanding of the rational structure of the universe, including the realm of values, was possible through an a priori deductive approach, the dominant note of the eighteenth century was a much humbler one. Reason was no longer looked upon as the "sum total of 'innate ideas' given prior to all experience which reveal the absolute essence of things,"[5] but was restricted to the world of phenomena. John Locke, Denis Diderot, or Voltaire no longer hopefully assumed that the fundamental problems of cosmic reality could be solved through human reason. All of this involved a conscious rejection of metaphysics. Nevertheless, no matter how vociferously eighteenth-century empiricists or nineteenth-century positivists repudiated metaphysics, their concepts of reason and science involved a thoroughly metaphysical assumption. Reason was not merely a methodological tool for reasoning or planning, but a normative concept and a guide to ultimate value. The universe was not an ethically indifferent world. Locke, Voltaire, Pierre Bayle, Jean Jacques Rousseau, Gotthold Lessing, and Immanuel Kant were all agreed that there was a rational ethics. From reason there followed axiomatically certain ethical conclusions, such as the rights and dignity of the individual or the categorical imperative.

[5] Ernst Cassirer, *The Philosophy of the Enlightenment*, tr. F. C. A. Koelln and J. P. Pettegrove (Princeton, N. J., 1951).

And although such eighteenth-century political thinkers as Frederick the Great and Benjamin Franklin might differ on the type of political institutions—absolutist, constitutional, or democratic—by which these ethical principles were best achieved, they generally agreed on what constituted a rational minimum ethics. Nor was this metaphysical element absent in the dominant nineteenth-century conceptions of science. For none of the important social philosophers in the positivistic tradition of the early or mid-nineteenth century was science a value-free method of inquiry as it was to become later for physical scientists like Albert Einstein or Max Planck or for cultural scientists like Max Weber. Science for Henri de Saint-Simon, Auguste Comte, John Stuart Mill, Henry Thomas Buckle, Karl Marx, Ludwig Büchner, Walter Bagehot, Herbert Spencer, or Hippolyte Taine was not merely a method, but also a system. Scientific inquiry would inevitably reveal the lawfulness of the universe and social science the lawfulness of society. For Pierre Proudhon, Condorcet, Comte, Marx, Mill, and Spencer, there was such a thing as a scientific or rational society. For most of these thinkers, the steady advance of the sciences became identical with the progress of society. And despite their great differences regarding the specific political and economic institutions reserved for the future, men as divergent as Condorcet, Marx, and Spencer were agreed on the general character of the normative, that is, scientific, society. For them the scientific study of society aimed at the discovery of general laws governing social movement, and these general laws were formulated as laws of social progress. History was seen as movement toward a normative society. In their best-known form, the laws of social movement were formulated in Comte's "Law of the Three Stages," but they appeared in similar forms in Turgot, Condorcet, Marx, Buckle, Spencer, and many other writers. More careful thinkers such as John Stuart Mill also recognized the tendency, but questioned whether at this point of empirical study one could speak of "laws of progress."[6] There was, however, gen-

---

[6] John Stuart Mill, *A System of Logic, Ratiocinative and Inductive, Being a Connected View of the Principles of Evidence and the Methods of Scientific Investigation* (7th ed., 2 vols., London, 1868), II, 510.

eral agreement regarding the steady accumulation of knowledge
and what was felt to be the progressive replacement of conjectural,
that is, theological or metaphysical, notions by scientific ones.
There was also broad agreement that this process was accompanied
by the steady growth of industry and the transformation of a
warlike society and its spirit into an industrial and pacific one.
There was further consensus that the course of history reflected
the steady decline of coercion in government and the increasing
role of rule by consent. As nineteenth-century social thought in
reaction to the French Revolution increasingly recognized the
role of impersonal social and historical forces, less emphasis was
placed on intellect as a moving force in historical change, and
progress was seen to an increasing extent as the result of an inner
logic of society. The belief in the basic harmony of science and
values, nevertheless, remained. Marx and Friedrich Engels, who
most vehemently asserted that their social theory was scientific
and free of moral presuppositions, also most insistently declared
that scientific analysis provided the key to the final, that is, the
scientific, normative social state of man. How widely spread the
belief in the scientific certainty of progress was even later in the
nineteenth century was demonstrated by the *Grand Larousse du
xixᵉ siècle*, which only a year after the national debacle of 1870–
1871 noted under the entry "Progress" that virtually all intelligent
men now accepted the idea.

As attempts at a scientific explanation of social phenomena, the
theories of progress stated as general laws of social development
proved to be untenable. As scientific theories they required empirical validation. None of the great theories of progress of the
nineteenth century were or could be validated. Despite their
scientific terminology, they remained speculative systems.[7]

In the decline of the faith in progress, nevertheless, the scientific
or logical critique of the idea was of relatively little importance.
Serious philosophical examination of the idea of progress came
largely only in the late nineteenth and the twentieth centuries,
when the idea had already lost much of its respectability. More

[7] For a discussion of the inadequacies of the idea of progress as a scientific
explanation of social phenomena, see, e.g., Karl Popper, *The Poverty of
Historicism* (London, 1957).

important was the critique of the conception of reason upon which the theories of progress had rested. This critique occurred in two stages. In its earlier form, to which we shall refer as "historism" for lack of a better term, the critics recognized the normative character of reason and the objective meaningfulness of the universe and of history, but insisted that reason in human matters was not universal and abstract but individual and concrete. In a later form, which Erich Kahler has called "historicism" to distinguish it from the earlier "historism,"[8] this critique led to ethical nihilism, to the position that there is no objective value in the universe or objective meaning in history, and that reason and science can therefore only tell us what *is*, even when they are describing value systems, but never what *ought to be*.[9]

Historism was the main competitor of the idea of progress in the early nineteenth century. The term, of course, needs definition. As we use the term here, perhaps somewhat arbitrarily because it has been given so many meanings,[10] it refers to an orientation rather than to a structured movement in German historical thought. Historism, as we use the term, signifies the position that history rather than nature is the key to truths and values. The nature of anything is contained in its history. Historism rejects the abstract concepts employed by philosophy and by the natural sciences as inadequate for rendering the concrete, living realities found within history. The theoretical foundations of historism are contained in the late eighteenth-century critique of natural law doctrine as found in Herder's early writings, especially in his *Also a Philosophy of History*. But on closer examination, the break between historism and the Enlightenment is not as profound as it first seems. Despite the insistence on the inadequacies of reason and the role of intuition in historical cognition, the main currents of historism were by no means antischolarly or even

[8] Erich Kahler, *The Meaning of History* (New York, 1964), 200.

[9] Cf. Arnold Brecht, *Political Theory: The Foundations of Twentieth-Century Political Thought* (Princeton, N. J., 1959).

[10] Cf. Dwight E. Lee and Robert N. Beck, "The Meaning of 'Historicism,'" *American Historical Review*, LIX (Apr. 1954), 568–77; cf. also *The Philosophy of History in Our Time: An Anthology*, ed. Hans Meyerhoff (New York, 1959), 10–11.

antiscientific. In a sense, the Enlightenment first made possible an objective, empirical approach to historical reality by freeing history from theology and thus making possible the study of history for its own sake. Historism indeed adopted the Enlightenment ideals of methodological correctness and tried to introduce the ideal of scientific objectivity into historical study. History as a scholarly discipline was born in large part under the impact of historism. But in another way, too, the historism of the early nineteenth century was still deeply rooted in the Enlightenment. It assumed that there was reason in history, either in the Hegelian sense that all history was the manifestation of reason, or in the sense of Johann Gottfried von Herder, Edmund Burke, or Leopold von Ranke, that behind the diversity of values and individdualities, there rested a divine will. "What happens is visible only in part in the world of senses," Wilhelm von Humboldt commented. "Every human individuality is only the phenomenal manifestation of an idea." And the "goal of history can only be the realization of the idea that mankind is to represent."[11] Similarly Ranke perceiving in the states something "real and spiritual at one and the same time [real-geistig]." States were not "passing conglomerations" but "spiritual substances, original creations of the human mind—I might say thoughts of God."[12]

In a very real sense this belief in the meaningfulness of the historical world led to an optimism that exceeded even that implied in the idea of progress. By seeing in the forces of history the will of God, historism tended to erase the dichotomy of what is and what ought to be. Every epoch was equally "immediate unto God."[13] Acting in terms of its great historical interests, the state for G. W. F. Hegel or Johann Gustav Droysen could not really sin.[14] "But seriously," Ranke had Friedrich, one of the characters

[11] Wilhelm von Humboldt, Über die Aufgabe des Geschichtschreibers (Berlin, 1822), 1, 17.

[12] Leopold von Ranke, "A Dialogue on Politics," in Theodore H. Von Laue, Leopold Ranke: The Formative Years (Princeton, N. J., 1950), 169; cf. Leopold von Ranke, Sämmtliche Werke (2d and 3d ed., 54 vols., Leipzig, 1875–90), IL/L, 329.

[13] Id., Weltgeschichte (9 vols., Leipzig, 1888–1902), IX Pt. II, 5.

[14] Cf. Johann Gustav Droysen, Historik: Vorlesungen über Enzyklopädie und Methodolgie der Geschichte, ed. Rudolf Hübner (Munich, 1937), 266.

in the "Dialogue on Politics," say, "you will be able to name few significant wars for which it could not be proved that genuine moral energy achieved the final victory."[15] The skepticism with which most natural law thinkers had regarded power was almost entirely lacking. The border line between historism and the idea of progress was often blurred. The affirmative historism of the nineteenth century did not involve as total a negation of the idea of progress as later writers have suggested;[16] it was rather the expression of confidence that all was basically well. The optimism of Droysen's *Historik*, Heinrich von Treitschke's *Deutsche Geschichte*, and even Friedrich Meinecke's *Weltbürgertum und Nationalstaat* was much more blatant than that of Ernest Renan's *L'Avenir de la science*, John Stuart Mill's *Essay on Liberty*, or Herbert Spencer's *The Man versus the State*.

The disenchantment with the optimism inherent in the idea of progress and in the earlier historism comes in stages, with the disillusionment following the French Revolution, the disappointments accompanying the Revolution of 1848, and the cultural malaise manifesting itself already very early in the nineteenth century in the consciousness of many writers such as Alexis de Tocqueville, John Stuart Mill, Sören Kierkegaard, and Aleksandr Herzen of the "crisis of modern civilization," a malaise that increased with the growth of a technological mass society. And although optimism remained dominant until the calamities of the First World War, and in America even later, the voices of cultural pessimism multiplied. The optimism of both the idea of progress and of historism was replaced by new orientations toward history. The cyclical theories of history have perhaps received more attention than they deserve in terms of their influence on modern thought or their value as scientifically defensible systems. Ernst von Lasaulx, Nikolai Danilevsky, Oswald Spengler, and Arnold Toynbee (in the first six volumes of the *Study of History*) have each in a brilliant work of synthesis developed a countersystem to the idea of progress. In place of a unilinear development, these writers have seen the history of man in terms of the

[15] Ranke, "Dialogue on Politics," 167.
[16] E.g., Helmuth Plessner, "Conditio Humana," in *Propyläen-Weltgeschichte* (10 vols., Frankfurt, 1960–), I, 33–86.

rise and fall of separate cultures. Each civilization was viewed in "morphological" terms, as a self-contained unit governed by inherent laws of growth and decline. The humanistic values of science, industry, equality, liberty, and humaneness which the adherents of the classical idea of progress had seen as rational norms and as the end products of history were now viewed as doomed.[17] These morphological systems were presented as scientific laws—by Toynbee as the result of supposed empirical investigation—and as such suffered all the logical weaknesses of the idea of progress. They remained speculative systems, lacking empirical validation. Their serious contribution lay rather in their attempt to analyze the nature of modern civilization. They raised the important question—although this is a question that was asked by Tocqueville, Mill, Jakob Burckhardt, Max Weber, and many others—whether the progress of civilization would not through the intellectualization and rationalization of life undermine the very values it had created.

Despite the pessimistic core of the cyclical theories, their denial of ultimate values, their insistence on the historicity of all cognition and all valuation, their rejection of the unity of human civilization, they nevertheless still affirmed the existence of structure and pattern, if not of meaning, in history. But even this became problematic in the course of the nineteenth century. The logical consequence of the secularization of thought was the collapse of the traditional theological and metaphysical concepts and the rise of the conception of nature as a purely impersonal, blind force devoid of purpose. The collapse of the belief in purpose in history did not follow directly upon the recognition that God is dead. Marx, Spencer, and Renan all viewed the world in naturalistic terms, and nevertheless failed to draw the ethical consequences of their atheistic or agnostic philosophical positions. The recognition that history had no structure or purpose and had only the meaning that men gave to it emerged only slowly in the nineteenth century, in Herzen, in Nietzsche, and in the epistemological debates of the German Neo-Kantians at the end of the

---

[17] See Georg G. Iggers, "The Idea of Progress in Recent Philosophies of History," *Journal of Modern History*, XXX (Sept. 1958), 215–26.

nineteenth century. But even Wilhelm Dilthey and Wilhelm Windelband were confident that the varieties of *Weltanschauungen* [world-outlooks], although rationally irreconcilable, reflected a fundamental cosmic unity. Heinrich Rickert stressed that the cultural sciences deal with values not as valid as such but as related to cultures, but even for him these values still appeared to possess reference to a transcendental ethics.[18] Only Max Weber among the Neo-Kantians drew the final conclusions of the historic position: that values were cultural phenomena with no reference to ultimate value. All values were rooted in *Weltanschauungen*, and *Weltanschauungen* were in the final analysis irrational. Man was thus faced by the ethical irrationality of the world and the insoluble conflict of the systems of values.[19] With this recognition, German historical thought had passed from historism, the faith that history is the sole key to value and reason, to historicism, the recognition that all values are historical and that "historical is identical with relative."[20]

Modern historicism had many sources, of course. It was not merely or primarily the outcome of the methodological and epistemological discussions of a small circle of German Neo-Kantian philosophers and cultural scientists. Anthropology, sociology, Marxism, Darwinism, Freudianism, the study of comparative religion, the naturalistic attitudes that accompanied the increasing role science played in the course of the nineteenth century, all helped to undermine the belief in objective value. Under the emotional impact of the First World War and its aftermath, these realizations became a dominant strain in Western historical thought. Not only were all values viewed as historical, but his-

---

[18] Heinrich Rickert, *Die Grenzen der naturwissenschaftlichen Begriffsbildung* (Tübingen, 1902), 736–38.

[19] See Max Weber, " 'Objectivity' in Social Science and Social Policy" and "The Meaning of 'Ethical Neutrality' in Sociology and Economics," in *The Methodology of the Social Sciences,* tr. Edward A. Shils and Henry A. Finch (Glencoe, Ill., 1949), see also Max Weber, "Science as a Vocation" and "Politics as a Vocation," in *From Max Weber: Essays in Sociology,* tr. H. H. Gerth and C. Wright Mills (New York, 1946).

[20] Ernst Troeltsch, *Die Absolutheit des Christentums und die Religionsgeschichte* (Tübingen, 1902), 49.

tory too was viewed now as "a tale told by an idiot" signifying nothing.[21]

The position that "history has no meaning,"[22] is shared today by thinkers coming from very different intellectual positions. It is a key concept in the existentialism of Jean-Paul Sartre, in the Protestant crisis theology of Karl Barth and of Reinhold Niebuhr, and in the positivism of Karl Popper. It denies not only the objectivity of value but also the coherence of history and for the existentialist position, at least, even the objectivity of method. Theodor Lessing's assertion that "history, originating in desires and volitions, needs and intentions, is a realization of the 'dream visions' of the human race . . . meaning of history is solely meaning which I give myself, and historical evolution is a development from myself to myself,"[23] is essentially as acceptable to the existentialist position as it is to Popper. History confronts us with facts, but "facts as such have no meaning," Popper reminds us; "they gain it only through our decisions."[24] And while it would not be correct to say that history has no meaning in Martin Heidegger's *Existenzphilosophie* [philosophy of existence], history ceases to have "objective meaning" for him because "objective meaning" presupposes that history confronts man as an object. To Heidegger, man is "thrown" into an ethically absurd universe in which, driven by care (*Sorge*) and anguish (*Angst*), confronted by death, he is forced to define himself. Within the framework of the concrete possibilities of the situation, man is confronted by a heritage that contained not one history but the "possibility of various histories." The individual "created" his history not on the basis of the objective happenings of the past, but by his decisions directed toward the future. What distinguishes Heidegger and such decisionist

[21] See Leo Strauss, *Natural Right and History* (Chicago, 1953), 18.

[22] Karl Popper, *The Open Society and Its Enemies* (2 vols., London, 1945), II, 264, 265. An exception to this position is found in Edward Hallett Carr, *What Is History? The George Macaulay Trevelyan Lectures Delivered in the University of Cambridge January–March 1961* (New York, 1962), an emphatic reassertion and redefinition of objectivity, meaning, and progress in history.

[23] Theodor Lessing, *Geschichte als Sinngebung des Sinnlosen* (2d ed., Munich, 1921), 10, quoted in Kahler, *Meaning of History*, 19–20.

[24] Popper, *Open Society and Its Enemies*, II, 265.

German thinkers of the 1920's as Ernst Jünger and Carl Schmitt[25] from Popper is that Heidegger, Jünger, and Schmitt opt against the humanistic and scholarly values of intellect, civilization, human welfare, and humaneness, and Popper opts for them, but Popper like Max Weber before him is aware of the element of faith in his decision.[26] Thus both for existentalist thought with its negative attitude toward intellect as well as for defenders of the scientific spirit such as Popper, history has no objective meaning. And with the death of meaning in history, the idea of progress is dead, too. Only in Communist countries does the idea of progress survive in an antiquated nineteenth-century form kept artificially alive by official policy.

The questions of value, meaning, and coherence in history are, nevertheless, not as easily disposed of as the literature leads us to believe. The basic assumption of the historicist position is, as José Ortega y Gasset has worded it, that "man has no nature but only history"[27] and that hence no rational ethics, no ethics based on human nature is possible. But is this really true?

Here is, of course, the heart of the difference between historism and historicism on the one hand and the doctrine of natural law on the other. Historism and historicism assumes that all is flux; natural law assumes that in the midst of change there is an element of stability in the lawful structure of the universe.

It is, of course, a great step from conceptions of the lawfulness of physical nature to those of human nature. A large number of thinkers who denied the possibility of objective or universally valid judgments in the cultural sciences have accepted them in the natural sciences. Men such as Heinrich Rickert, Karl Mannheim, and Popper were willing to recognize in nature what they were unwilling to admit in history: objective coherence. If nature is coherent, then natural science is possible. Although every scientific theory is merely a system of symbols that only indirectly

[25] See Christian Graf von Krockow, *Die Entscheidung: Eine Untersuchung über Ernst Jünger, Carl Schmitt, Martin Heidegger* (Stuttgart, 1958).

[26] Popper, *Open Society and Its Enemies*, II, 265.

[27] José Ortega y Gasset, *Obras Completas* (9 vols., Madrid, 1953–62), VI, 41.

and inaccurately conceptualizes "reality," it nevertheless refers to an objective coherence. There is thus a norm in scientific research that we call truth even if we can never perfectly attain it. And connected with this norm is another norm closely related to it; this we may call methodological correctness. All this has a direct relevance to the idea of progress because these norms provide the criteria of progress in the sciences. Even in the age of historicism, few thinkers would agree with Oswald Spengler that all systems of science and mathematics have no truth values beyond the cultures to which they relate.[28] And even Spenglerians are forced to act as if they lived in a world governed by an objective physical order.

But not only is there coherence in the physical world; there also appears to be a degree of coherence in that area of history which we call the history of science. The historistic admonition that *individuum est ineffabile* [the individual thing is ineffable], that it is the task of the historian not to judge, but merely to show *wie es eigentlich gewesen* [how it actually happened], that every epoch is "immediate unto God" is clearly inadequate in the history of science. We are dealing not merely with the variety of scientific views but with theories of greater or lesser truth value. The existence of coherence in nature makes progress in scientific knowledge theoretically possible. It is, of course, impossible at this stage (or probably ever) to validate a law of progress in scientific knowledge such as Comte postulated, but we can observe more or less clearly definable trends. This does not exclude reversal. The heliocentric theory and the circulation of the blood, both known to Hellenistic science, had to be "rediscovered" in modern times. Nevertheless, the reality of objective coherence to an extent guides the direction of scientific inquiry. It makes it possible, moreover, to draw lines of development. It also means that the historian is not confronted by a multiplicity of equally meaningless facts, as Popper suggested, but by facts of greater or lesser significance. The selection of these facts in the writing of

[28] See Oswald Spengler, *The Decline of the West* (2 vols., New York, n.d.), I, Chap. 11, "The Meaning of Numbers."

the history of science is no longer left entirely to the subjective decision of the historian.

What is true of the history of science is also true of the history of technology. But here we are not yet on very controversial ground. For much of historicist theory would admit the possibility of civilizational (scientific, technical, even organizational) progress, but not of cultural (spiritual or moral) progress. This, of course, involves the question whether there is a "human nature" and the even more difficult question whether there are generally applicable norms that derive from this human nature.

To an extent, of course, we shall probably all agree, despite Ortega y Gasset and Sartre's stand to the contrary, that there is a minimal common basis of human nature not only on a biological but also on a psychological level. In a sense existentialist philosophy which has insisted so forcefully that "there is no human nature"[29] has paradoxically itself traveled on the road back to the recognition of a common human nature, at least in its extreme preoccupation with the "human condition" in which we all share. *Sorge, Dasein zum Tode, Angst, Nausée* [care, being-towards-death, anxiety, nausea] are all states that are universally human rather than in Herder's words "national . . . and individual."[30] The practicing historian, no matter how committed to historistic principles, has never been able to escape the assumption of a constancy in human nature. For what was the critical method in history of which the nineteenth-century historians were so proud but the insistence on the recognition of the coherence of physical nature in the case of the criteria of external criticism and of human nature in relation to the principles of internal criticism. As W. H. Walsh suggested:

"It was generalizations about human nature which ultimately lay behind historical explanations . . . we could not even begin to understand [the past], unless we presupposed some propositions

---

[29] Sartre, *Existentialism.*

[30] Johann Herder, *Auch eine Philosophie der Geschichte zur Bildung der Menschheit*, in *Sämmtliche Werke*, ed. Bernhard Suphan (33 vols., Berlin, 1877–1913), V, 505.

about human nature, unless we applied some notion of what is reasonable or normal in human behavior."[31]

Again, if we look at the history of institutions, we see certain lines of continuity. The Saint-Simonians formulated as a social law the ever-widening circle of association of man in the course of history from family to city, nation, church, and finally world state.[32] We can hardly speak of law, and even less of progress in a valuative sense, but we are nevertheless confronted by an observable trend, by what Kahler has called "the gradual expansion of existential scope," an "evolution, not to be confounded with progress, which has a moral or merely functional connotation— . . . from the tribe to city and city-state" to feudal principalities, territorial estates, dynastic and nation-states, popular nations "to civilizational and ideological power blocs, and finally to the technically, technologically prepared 'one world' which is humanly, psychologically, very far from organized realization, but which looms as the only alternative that science and technology have presented us to their opposite achievement, nuclear or biological annihilation."[33] Other trends are equally observable. Max Weber has spoken of a continuous process of intellectualization and rationalization of life since the beginnings of civilization in the ancient Near East.[34] In a similar vein, Kahler observes the steady "secularization, rationalization, scientification and technicalization" of human existence.[35]

These trends do not necessarily represent progress in so far as we mean by progress development toward more moral institutions and more moral man. They may constitute change rather than improvement, change which in the growing rationalization of life may actually be undermining the very values that the classical theorists of progress regarded as the criteria of progress. More-

---

[31] W. H. Walsh, *An Introduction to Philosophy of History* (5th ed., London, 1958), 107. For a similar line of reasoning, see Carr, *What Is History?* 122–23.

[32] See *The Doctrine of Saint-Simon: An Exposition, First Year, 1828–1829*, tr. Georg G. Iggers (Boston, 1958), 60–61.

[33] Kahler, *Meaning of History*, 195–96.

[34] Weber, "Science as a Vocation."

[35] Kahler, *Meaning of History*, 196.

over, we are admittedly confronted by the methodological problem of measuring these "trends."

We come closer to the problem of values when we deal with another set of trends that appear to be operating in modern society. Condorcet predicted the disappearance of slavery, the rise of literacy, the diminution of inequalities among the sexes, reforms of prison codes, and the decline of poverty. Again one can hardly deny that these trends have operated during the past 175 years, although it is difficult to measure them. We are, of course, dealing with trends over a relatively short span of time, which may conceivably be reversed either catastrophically through thermonuclear warfare or through the very contradictions within society that these social developments, considered beneficial by Condorcet, may have created. The future may correspond more closely to George Orwell's 1984 than to Edward Bellamy's Boston of the year 2000. Certainly we have in the course of the twentieth century approached Orwell's 1984 in many ways, but we have approximated Bellamy's Boston in even more ways.

In rereading the optimistic literature of the late eighteenth and of the nineteenth centuries we are impressed both by how right the prophets of those days were and how wrong they were. Condorcet, Saint-Simon, Mill, and Spencer all underestimated the role of evil. "No one, whose opinion deserves a moment's consideration," Mill writes, "can doubt that most of the positive evils of the world are in themselves removable, and will, if human affairs continue to improve, be in the end reduced within narrow limits."[36] They overconfidently predicted the disappearance of war and tyranny. But they were right in many other ways. For, on the whole, the modern world has moved in the direction that the optimists of the Enlightenment and of the nineteenth century predicted. We need only reopen a book like Taine's *Notes on England* in the 1870's or the Quaker report on the condition of the colored population of Philadelphia in 1849 to be reminded how widespread and how severe was the spiritual and material degradation existing a century ago. Not that such degradation does not exist today even

[36] John Stuart Mill, "Utilitarianism," in *The Philosophy of John Stuart Mill*, ed. Marshall Cohen (New York, 1961), 339.

in the technologically more developed countries, but for the first time we can envisage the radical decline of disease, ignorance, and poverty throughout the entire world. Barring a world war, we may safely predict the continued increase in levels of health, education, and welfare throughout the world, at least in the foreseeable future.

Certainly we cannot formulate a law of progress in the sense in which Comte and Buckle sought such laws. The very complexity of human society makes it doubtful that quantitative formulations similar to those developed in the natural sciences will ever be of more than restricted use in the cultural sciences. There is no certainty that the trends we have described will not be reversed. Moreover, we may be accused of having chosen values by which to measure progress that have no basis in human nature as such, but are merely the products of a time or of our subjective decisions. Finally, it may be argued again that the very values of modern civilization that we have identified as progressive may lead to their own destruction.

This brings us back to the question of whether there are real norms by which historical change can be measured. The idea of progress, rooted in the doctrine of natural law, assumed that there were. It assumed that there was a human nature, that the end of human life was happiness, that the full achievement of happiness for man involved the full delevopment of his rational as well as his physical potentialities,[37] and that the structure of human nature therefore gave the moral world a degree of rational coherence. The core of this ethics was summed up in the doctrine of natural rights, in the belief in the right of the individual to his person. This assumed that violation of these rights, as constituted by murder, slavery, or exploitation, represented objective wrongs. Neither Locke, nor Voltaire, nor Kant attempted to prove the existence of such rights by reason. They considered them to be self-evident truths, data known through direct ethical intuition, conditions of human consciousness.[38]

Was the Enlightenment belief in a rational ethics mere wishfulness, or did it possess a basin in reality? Is there below the pattern

[37] *Ibid.*, 331.
[38] See Alfred Cobban, *The Crisis of Civilization* (London, 1941), 108–109.

of diverse customs and manners a basic substratum of human values? Historism has denied this. Related to this problem is the question of whether there is such a thing as mental health. Are there criteria of mental normalcy, or is normalcy merely a statistical concept relative to a given culture? May we speak of a sane society, as Erich Fromm has? Was Nazi Germany merely a different or a sick society? Was Auschwitz merely an instrument of policy or of immorality? Is the murderer merely a man with a different morality or a morally sick man?

If there are norms of morality deriving from human nature, or even merely norms of mental health, then there exists the theoretical possibility of a normal society. We may then conceivably in the moral and social world be confronted by something resembling the progress in the sciences and technology, by a tendency to achieve greater rationality. We may then perhaps see in the great revolutionary movements of modern history the groping toward morally more rational institutions, even though there are reverses and we can discern no clear or predetermined pattern.

All of this must be said with extreme caution. We are not dealing with a movement that as yet (or perhaps ever) can be formulated as a general social law, as certain of the nineteenth-century advocates of the theory of progress had believed possible. We are dealing at most with certain observable trends about whose direction there can be disagreement. And even if we agree that society has moved toward greater intellectualization, equality, and wealth, we may question whether such a movement has been beneficial to man or whether, as cultural pessimists from Kierkegaard to Ortega y Gasset have suggested, it has merely emptied man of his spiritual substance and laid the foundations for the most systematic tyranny of man over man. How can we speak of progress in a moral sense in the age of totalitarianism and total war? The Final Solution, which in a sense symbolized the high point of the application of modern science and technology in the service of inhumanity, appears to spell the total absurdity of progress. Gerhard Ritter, Meinecke, and many others have suggested that the roots of the Nazi Revolution were to be found in the rationalistic and equalitarian beliefs of the French Revolution and in the breakdown of religious beliefs and traditional class structures. The growing concern with economic welfare, which Comte and Spencer had hailed, Ritter saw as a major contributing factor to modern barbarism. But was Nazism really a phenomenon of the "failure of modern mass democracy" as Ritter suggested?[39] Was it not in an important way the revolt of an atavistic political romanticism against the conditions of modern society in a country in which, Ritter and Meinecke notwithstanding, Enlightenment values and democratic institutions were underdeveloped, in which the gap between modern realities and premodern attitudes and class structure was much greater than in most Western democratic countries?

It was the great failing of the prophets of progress that they underestimated the extent of man's destructiveness and irrationality. The failing of historism and of historicism has been in misunderstanding the role of rationality and morality in human behavior. We can accept the idea of progress today only with serious qualifications. Progress as yet is only a hypothesis and a very questionable one. The reality of human evil, as Reinhold Niebuhr has suggested, makes the attainment of any perfect social state impossible. The complexities of history, in which, as Löwith pointed out, conscious human action always has results other than those intended,[40] make calculated progress much more problematic than the great believers in social engineering of the last century had believed. As Popper has warned us, the idea of progress as a "belief in Inexorable Laws of Historical Destiny" has led to the sacrifice of countless men and women upon the altar of totalitarian fanaticism.[41] While progress seems to be invalidated as a universal idea, there is, nevertheless, a rational basis to the belief that within limited spheres man's actions can create more rational conditions. Despite the strong currents of cultural pessimism that have marked our age, the social policies of all nations have proceeded on the assumption that within limited, defined goals, planned progress is

---

[39] See Gerhard Ritter, "The Fault of Mass Democracy," in *The Nazi Revolution: Germany's Guilt or Germany's Fate?* ed. John Snell (Boston, 1959), 76–84; cf. Friedrich Meinecke, *The German Catastrophe: Reflections and Recollections*, tr. Sidney B. Fay (Cambridge, Mass., 1950).

[40] Karl Löwith, "Die Dynamik der Geschichte und der Historismus," *Eranos-Jahrbuch*, XXI (1952), 217–54.

[41] See the dedication to Popper's *Poverty of Historicism*.

possible. And the goals of this progress, except where they have turned toward war and repression, have remained the classical values of the Enlightenment: the improvement of education, health, welfare, and individual dignity. The programs of aid to underdeveloped countries have underlined to what extent modern civilization, despite its negative aspects, has been regarded in both the Western as well as the non-Western countries as a positive good, not only in a material, but also in a spiritual sense. Indeed, the twentieth century, which has seen the decline of the idea of progress as a respectable theory of history, has also witnessed the idea more firmly established as a working assumption of public policy than it ever was in the optimistic century that preceded it.[42]

In conclusion, we must frankly admit that the idea of progress is untenable as a scientific explanation of historical movement. The theory is not, however, without rational foundations and deserves much more serious re-examination than it has received in recent thought. And independent of its role as a cognitive theory regarding the nature of history, the idea of progress must also be viewed as an ethical hypothesis that assumes, rationally or on faith, the reality of positive values and the meaningfulness of ethical behavior.

[42] Carr in *What Is History?* notes an "expansion of reason" (p. 190) in the twentieth century and optimistically interprets the increase in social and economic planning as "an advance in the application of reason to human affairs, an increased capacity in man to understand and master himself and his environment, which I should be prepared, if necessary, to call by the old-fashioned name of progress" (pp. 188–89).

PART SIX

Progress Reaffirmed

1   *Charles Frankel*

*An eloquent witness for the defense in the trial of the idea of prog-
ress is Charles Frankel (1917-   ), especially in his book* The Case for
Modern Man, *published in 1955. Professor of Philosophy at Columbia
University and the author also of an important study of the eighteenth-century idea of progress, Frankel in this excerpt from* The
Case for Modern Man *assails Reinhold Niebuhr's interpretation of
progressivist doctrine on the subject of human fallibility.*

Liberalism, it is said on all sides, has forgotten to take human
egoism into account, and has been utopian in its conception of
what can be made of man. This picture of liberalism has become
one of the standing commonplaces of current discussion, and is
shared by the New Liberal and the New Conservative alike. "Practically all schools of modern culture," says Mr. Niebuhr, ". . . are
united in denying the obvious fact that all men are persistently
inclined to regard themselves more highly and are more assid-
uously concerned with their own interests than any 'objective'
view of their importance would warrant." But the belief in the undying egoism of human beings, and the persistence in any society of the struggle for power, has in fact been the distinguishing
feature of the liberal approach to politics. "The principle of human nature, upon which the necessity of government is founded,
the propensity of one man to possess himself of the objects of
desire at the cost of another, leads on, by infallible sequence, not
only to that degree of plunder which leaves the members (except
the instruments and recipients) the bare means of subsistence, but
to that degree of cruelty which is necessary to keep in existence
the most intense terrors." These are not Mr. Niebuhr's words.
They are the words of James Mill, the liberal and utilitarian, writing on the foundations of government. The idea that philosophical

SOURCE. Charles Frankel, *The Case for Modern Man*, New York: Harper
& Row, 1955, pp. 101–108. Copyright 1955, 1956 by Charles Frankel. Reprinted by permission of Harper & Row, Publishers and the author.

liberalism has been committed to a perfectionist theory of human nature is in fact a parody of liberal thought.

In general, the British liberal tradition has taken most of its ideas on the behavior of political man from Thomas Hobbes, who described man as *homo lupus*—a predatory animal. Even those figures who, like John Locke, have taken a more genial view of human nature, have nevertheless regarded the irrepressible tendency of each man to favor his own cause as a major reason for substituting a politically organized society for "the state of nature." And in the twentieth century, that arch exemplar of liberalism in thought and action, Bertrand Russell, has tried to base an entire political theory on the strength, uneliminability, and remarkable variety of men's demands for power. Nor is it only British liberalism that does not fit the portrait that is now drawn of classic liberalism. The philosophers of the French Enlightenment are repeatedly described as boundless optimists and visionaries. But is it really possible to say of Rousseau who wrote the *Confessions*, or Diderot who wrote *Rameau's Nephew*, or Voltaire who wrote *Candide*, that they entertained great illusions either about their own goodness or the goodness of other men? Even the philosopher Helvetius, who was most extreme in his hopes about what could be done with human nature, and who was looked upon as a little strange by most of his liberal contemporaries, wrote: "In order to love mankind, we must expect little from them."

What, then, is the reason for the belief that modern liberalism has traditionally entertained exaggeratedly optimistic notions about human nature? There are two apparent bits of evidence. If we take Condorcet's *Outline of the Progress of the Human Mind*, the book which, more than any other, exemplifies the classic liberal interpretation of history, we find in it two central theses. One is the idea of "the perfectibility of man." The other is the belief that human happiness and virtue will be augmented with the progress of knowledge. Let us see whether Condorcet's argument in this book necessarily implies an innocent conception of human nature.

Condorcet wrote *The Progress of the Human Mind* while he was in hiding from the Jacobin Terror. It is one of the classic testaments of faith to be found in Western literature, and is essentially a religious book—a reflection, in the face of death, on what is mortal and what is immortal in human life. And what is immortal, Condorcet affirmed, is the progress of the human mind, and the consequent indefinite perfectibility of mankind. To participate in this enterprise of progress is to participate in something which gives an undying point of reference to human affairs; and to contemplate the spectacle of progress is to be redeemed from the vanities and consoled for the sufferings to which human existence is heir. Condorcet has regularly been singled out as the very model of the woolly-headed liberal transported by an impossible dream. But the idea that a belief in the indefinite perfectibility of mankind exhibits a naïvely optimistic view of human affairs comes from a simple failure to understand (or perhaps to read) what Condorcet actually said on this subject. The phrase, "the indefinite perfectibility of mankind," is ambiguous, and can be easily—not to say eagerly—misinterpreted. But on the question of what this phrase means Condorcet took great trouble to be precise and clear.

What, asks Condorcet, is the extent of the improvement in the human situation for which we may legitimately hope? What does it mean to say that man is "indefinitely perfectible"? Condorcet raises this question specifically in connection with his prediction that in the future the average life expectancy of human beings will be steadily increased. "Doubtless," he writes, "man will never become immortal." But "the progress of preventive medicine, more healthful food and lodging, a way of life that will develop the body through proper exercise without damaging it by overwork, and, finally, the destruction of the two most active causes of physical degeneracy, extreme poverty and extreme wealth," can be expected to bring "a time when death shall be no more than the result of extraordinary accidents or of the ever more gradual decay of the vital forces." Now, is there any limit which can be set to this process?

Condorcet answers this question by introducing an important distinction between two meanings of the term "limit." It is a distinction which his critics wholly overlook.

"The average length of life [he writes] may grow either in accordance with a law by which it continually approaches a certain definite magnitude without ever reaching it, or in accordance with a law by which the length of life, in the long course of the ages, steadily surpasses every determinate figure which has been assigned to it as a limit. In the latter case, such growth would be truly indefinite, in the strictest sense of the word, because there would exist no bounds which it cannot pass. In the former case, however, it would be indefinite *for us*, since we cannot state the limit which this growth must forever approach but cannot absolutely reach; and this is particularly the case if we only know that this increase in the length of human life is endless, and cannot even· say in which of the two senses of 'indefinite' this term is applicable to it. This is precisely the state of our present knowledge concerning the perfectibility of the human species. Such is the sense in which we can call this perfectibility 'indefinite.' "

In short, there is nothing utopian about Condorcet's conception of indefinite progress. He does not assert that there are no limits to human hopes. He merely asserts that we can never say that we have reached these limits. This is a point in which he is in total agreement with Mr. Niebuhr.[1] Mr. Niebuhr's quarrel with the doctrine of the indefinite perfectibility of man is a quarrel he has invented for himself. The principle of the indefinite perfectibility of man is simply the denial that there are any absolutes which the human mind can safely affirm. It is not a prediction about the future; it is the statement of a policy for guiding human behavior —a policy of putting the *status quo* on the defensive, and of refusing to decide in advance that any given problem is beyond the power of human beings to solve.

Let us turn now to Condorcet's belief that progress in knowledge promotes virtue. As his account of how men in the past used their knowledge to exploit their fellows suggests, Condorcet rec-

---

[1] Mr. Niebuhr writes, "Actually human power over nature and history is both limited and limitless. It is limited in the sense that all individual and collective forms of life are subject to mortality. No human achievements can annul man's subjection to natural finitude. But human power is also limitless in the sense that no fixed limits can be set for the expansion of human capacities."

ognized that knowledge gave men powers that could be used for better or worse. But in talking about "the progress of knowledge," he meant among other things the *diffusion* of knowledge; and he did believe that this would promote virtue. But it was not because knowledge necessarily makes the man who possesses it more virtuous. It is because knowledge makes that man better able to protect himself against other men's vices. Condorcet's belief that the diffusion of knowledge would improve human behavior rested essentially on the common-sense assumption that if men have enough information to know what is going on and how their own interests are affected, the inveterate egoism, greed, and cupidity of their rulers could be more easily controlled. The practical, political application of the idea that diffusion of knowledge leads to moral progress is not in the development of a "scientific system of morality," but in plans for public education, for the development of a free press, and for the maintenance of civil liberties. And if the moral progress which Condorcet envisaged has not taken place to the degree he expected, this does not prove that moral progress does not follow from the diffusion of knowledge. It may only indicate the development of social conditions which make the diffusion of knowledge extraordinarily difficult. Condorcet did not foresee the emergence of such conditions. But he was not wrong to believe that it should be a basic objective of a liberal society to work for their avoidance. And to talk about the wickedness of man as though it were uncontrollable merely diverts attention from this issue.

If we judge the liberal philosophy of history by its most representative spokesman, the belief in the progress of man was not made up out of whole cloth, and the men who held it were not suffering from an *idée fixe* about human goodness which prevented them from recognizing plain facts. In Condorcet's hands, the belief in the perfectibility of man was really a belief better translated into English as a belief in the *improvability* of man. And the ideals it projected point the way to our crucial problems, and give us a framework that is still valid for our social thinking.

That Condorcet's enthusiasm was aroused by this vision, and that many liberal writers in the eighteenth and nineteenth centuries (and an even greater number of illiberal ones) were stimulated by it into utopian or quasi-utopian dreams is undeniable. They lived in the fine glow of a major revolution in human affairs, and they recognized this revolution for what it was. If they were overly optimistic, it was a matter of mood and temper and circumstance. It was not a matter of fundamental philosophic principle. To take a patronizing attitude toward the men who held these dreams is to reveal a failure of historical imagination. For these men were living through a scientific and technological revolution which gave promise that for the first time in human history men would be able to get off their backs in the struggle with nature—that men could finally, to put it in unadorned terms, eat adequately and live in reasonable comfort and health. To have been dazzled by the prospects which this revolution held forth is not only understandable; more, the men who were dazzled, and who wrote the passages at which the New Pessimists now scoff, were performing the important function of announcing the new possibilities for the moral and intellectual improvement of mankind which this very real material revolution had set loose. In the light of what was contained in human experience up to that time, to do this took courage and imagination; and not to have done it would have been a greater error, a more sizable failure to provide directing ideas to modern culture, than to have played the old tune of original sin.

There is, in fact, a quite fundamental confusion in the idea that the liberal doctrine of "the goodness of man" reveals an impossibly naïve theory of human nature. It it a confusion between a scheme of moral values and a psychological theory. The slogan, "the goodness of man," is indeed an alternative to the doctrine of original sin. But it is not primarily an alternative description of human behavior; it is an alternative frame of moral reference—a dramatic device for freeing practical questions of politics or historical explanation from control by the ideal of salvation and the value judgments that follow from it.

For the doctrine of original sin defines "good" and "evil" with respect to the final goal of personal salvation. By calling man "evil" or "sinful," it means to say that man, through his own efforts alone, cannot be immortal, or free his mind or soul from dependence on a corrupt body, or be infallible in his intellectual judgments, or perfectly saintly in his behavior. And liberal philosophers would have agreed with all of these statements of fact. What they were doing in speaking about "the goodness of man" was simply to assert the legitimacy of talking about human traits in some other context than this context of sin and redemption. From the point of view of being saved from sin, for example, egoism might be evil; but from an economic point of view it might be good as a pivot for ambition; or from a political point of view it might be good as a defense against despotism; or, indeed, it might be neither good nor bad, but simply what has to be taken into account in governing human affairs. "Moralists declaim continually against the badness of men," wrote Helvetius, "but this shows how little they understand of this matter. Men are not bad; they are merely subject to their own interests." It is this "transvaluation of values," this introduction of a new context for the assessment of human traits, which is involved in statements about "the goodness of man."

It is Mr. Niebuhr's failure to see this point which explains his caricature of liberal views of human nature. On Mr. Niebuhr's accounting, Hobbes and Locke, Hume and Rousseau, rationalists and romantics, all turn out to have entertained essentially the same overestimate of the "goodness" of man. But it is plain that if there is anything that unites these men, it is not a psychological theory, nor even a common set of value judgments; it is only a common disposition to place whatever value judgments they make in a humanistic setting, to refuse to impose standards on man which are irrelevant to what he wants and what he can do. The liberal attack on the doctrine of original sin was a phase in the transition of social thinking from preoccupation with the classic problem of "theodicy"—the justification of God's ways to man—to a preoccupation with concrete, individual problems in morals and society. It set the problem of man's transcendent perversity aside; it set the problem of man's other-worldly destiny aside; it dropped the question of salvation out of the group of questions which must be examined before a social program can be developed. In arguing for the possibility of greater happiness in human affairs, philosophical liberals were not talking about redemption through history. They were not talking about redemption at all. For "happiness" is not a synonym for "salvation," and "progress" is not a synonym for the journey of the soul to God.

2 Arnold J. Toynbee

Down to 1939 and the publication of the fourth, fifth, and sixth volumes of A Study of History, *Arnold J. Toynbee (1889-) would have to be numbered among the leading opponents of the faith in progress in modern times. Like his German predecessor Oswald Spengler, he had put forward a cyclical theory of history, which held that civilizations rise and fall according to a definite pattern and that our own Western civilization might expect to go the way of all the others. In the postwar years, however, Toynbee has superimposed on his cyclicalism certain clearly progressivist ideas: the last six volumes of his* Study, *1954-1961, develop a conception of the general religious progress of mankind and resurrect the doctrine of man's ultimate perfectibility. In this selection from the twelfth volume, Toynbee unites the Christian hope of man's spiritual redemption and the faith of the Enlightenment in the efficacy of sociopolitical reform. In Toynbee's current judgment, the historic civilizations may all be doomed, but mankind has an opportunity to rise above them to a new, planetary level of existence.*

In earlier volumes of this book I have compared the situation of mankind in the present age to a climber's pitch. Below us lies the ledge that our pre-human ancestors reached in the act of becoming human. In the Age of the Civilizations mankind has been making a

SOURCE. Arnold J. Toynbee, "The Next Ledge," from *A Study of History*, Volume XII: *Reconsiderations*, New York: Oxford University Press, 1961, pp. 562–572. Copyright 1961 by Oxford University Press. Reprinted by permission of Oxford University Press and the author.

number of attempts to scale the cliff-face that towers up from the ledge reached by Primitive Man. The next ledge above, unlike the ledge immediately below, is invisible to climbers who are striving to reach it. All that they know is that they feel compelled to risk their necks in the hope of gaining this next ledge and in the faith that the endeavour is worth while.

This simile is a myth in the Platonic usage of the word. . . . Myths are unenlightening if they do not transcend experience, and unwarrantable if they contradict it. My myth of the climber's pitch is, I should say, in accord with mankind's experience in the Age of the Civilizations. The civilizations themselves are movements; they are purposeful movements aiming at an objective; and they are not the only movements of the kind in the span of human history that is within our ken. They were preceded by a series of earlier new departures in which mankind's pace gradually accelerated and its impetus slowly gathered momentum. Moreover, within less than two thousand five hundred years of the date of the emergence of the earliest of the civilizations, the earliest of the higher religions appeared and, in appearing, stepped up the impetus to a still higher degree. After the World had suffered the shock of the First World War, Smuts remarked[1] that "the tents have been struck and the great caravan of humanity is once more on the march". This was true of the generation of which it was said; but it is no less true of all previous generations of which there is any surviving record.

Though the goal of mankind's continuous and increasing endeavours is still hidden below our horizon, we know, nevertheless, what it is. We can discern it, without having to divine the future, by looking inwards; for mankind's goal is written large in the constitution of human nature. What changed our pre-human ancestors into human beings like ourselves was the acquisition of consciousness and will.[2] These two spiritual faculties are human

[1] J. C. Smuts: *The League of Nations: A Practical Suggestion* (London 1918, Hodder & Stoughton), p. 71.

[2] The reality of human freedom is recognized by people who differ widely from each other in their account of it. 'The rationalists will . . . admit, probably, that, within certain biological limits, Man is free. This freedom, however, is not, to them, the freedom of "the law of God", nor is it evidence

nature's distinguishing marks; and their character is ambivalent. They are both a treasure that gives us hope and a burden that puts us in peril. Their emergence in Man has split the unity of the Universe, and broken its harmony, for every conscious, wilful, human soul. The price of human knowledge and freedom is an intellectual and a moral relativity. Each of us sees the Universe divided between himself and all the rest of it; and each of us seeks to make himself the centre round which all the rest shall revolve. This constitution of human nature sets human nature's goal. Its goal is to transcend the intellectual and moral limitations that its relativity imposes on it. Its intellectual goal is to see the Universe as it is in the sight of God, instead of seeing it with the distorted vision of one of God's self-centred creatures. Human nature's moral goal is to make the self's will coincide with God's will, instead of pursuing self-regarding purposes of its own.

Few, if any, human souls have been entirely unaware of this goal or entirely indifferent to it. The saints have dedicated them-selves to the pursuit of it, and some saints have come within a hair's breadth of attaining it—as it has seemed to spectators of ordinary spiritual stature, though never to the spiritual athletes themselves. The value of the goal lies in the goal itself; and there-fore the goal cannot be attained unless it is pursued for its own sake. But, since the wages of sin is death, and this truth is con-tinually being attested by experience, there has always been a utilitarian incentive, as well as a disinterested motive, for conduct that, when disinterested, is righteous. In our day this utilitarian consideration has become pressing, owing to a sudden immense increase in the power that knowledge and freedom have been accumulating in human hands. The human power that has in-creased is not a human soul's power over itself. There is no evi-dence of any increase in that within the time over which our records extend. So far as one can guess, human beings are no better, and saints are no more frequent, in the present-day world than they will have been in, let us say, the Lower Palaeolithic

of the intervention of anything supernatural in human affairs. This freedom is a biological phenomenon, purely and simply' (M. Savelle in *The Pacific Historical Review*, vol. xxv, No. 1 (February, 1956), pp. 56–67).

Age. The power that has been accumulating and increasing is collective power over both human souls and non-human nature. Now that mankind's collective power is within sight of becoming able to extinguish all human life, and perhaps all life of any kind on the face of the planet, the works of righteousness are being demanded of us urgently, not only for their own sake, but by our concern for self-preservation.

For approaching this objective we might seem to have a choice between two roads: one rough and narrow, the other smooth and broad. The hard way of doing the works of righteousness is to be righteous. It is hard, but it is unquestionably open, since it is the way that is followed by the saints. The easy way would be to be 'conditioned' to be incapable of choosing to do anything else. This is the way of the social insects on Earth—or of the angels in Heaven if we prefer to speak the language of Christian mythology. Till within living memory this bee-like or angelic way of doing righteous acts willy-nilly was not open to the human race. The possibility of "conditioning" human souls, like the possibility of genocide, has appeared above Man's horizon within our own life-time. When Aldous Huxley's *Brave New World* was published in 1932, the notion of "brain-washing" was still little more than an anti-Utopian flight of fancy. By 1961 it had become part of mankind's evergrowing repertory of accomplishments. Considering that these two portentous new crimes—genocide and "conditioning"—had become feasible simultaneously, mankind might be strongly tempted to seek security against genocide by acquiescing in 'conditioning'. If it were a question of choosing between the two evils, it would be difficult for human beings to decide that the self-annihilation of their own race was the lesser evil of the two. To be "conditioned" would be likely to seem a less terrible option than to be extinguished; and, even if "conditioning" were not commended by presenting itself at the only practical alternative to extinction,[3] it would have an attrac-

---

[3] It can also commend itself insidiously by masquerading as its own antithesis: self-determination. F. A. Hayek makes the point that the demand for conscious control or direction of social purposes means, in effect, a demand for giving some single mind and will the control over all others. It means this, in Hayek's view, because ' "conscious" and "deliberate" are terms which

tion in itself for beings saddled with the burden of consciousness and will. This burden, inherent in human nature, is a grievous one. We are born with it on our backs; and it condemns us to serve a life-sentence of tension and struggle. If we could get rid of it, we could relax and rest. And, if the power to get rid of it has now at last come within our reach, why should we not avail ourselves of it? The burden has been imposed on us without our leave being asked. What obligation have we to go on putting up with it when once we have learnt how to relieve ourselves of it? The attraction of "conditioning" is akin to the attraction of drugs and intoxicants.

One specious argument in favour of submitting to being "conditioned" would be that, after all, this would not be an entirely new departure. Should we be doing anything more novel or more questionable than just carrying to its logical conclusion a human practice that must be as old as, or older than, mankind itself? Human society may be inconceivable without conscious and deliberate agreement, but it is also hardly conceivable without the bond of habit; and, if it is true that our pre-human ancestors could hardly have managed to become human beings without having been social animals already, habit must always have been one of the key-institutions of human life. Our habits are inculcated by our education. This, taken in the broad sense, is a life-long social drill. It teaches us to perform by mimesis, without reasoning why, all kinds of acts that we should never have dreamed of if we had been left to ourselves. Between drilling and "conditioning" is there any great gulf? Could not "conditioning" be fairly described as being social drill that is made infallibly effective by being given a final twist to clinch it?

This argument is rebutted by a series of counter-considerations. It may be true that human beings have not been able to maintain

have meaning only when applied to individuals' (*The Counter-Revolution of Science*, p. 87). There is, however, surely the alternative possibility that a conscious and deliberate control may be exercised jointly by a number of minds and wills achieving and maintaining agreement with each other. If this were not possible, there could be no such thing as human society. For this, unlike insect society, is not a product of automatic instinctive behaviour.

society without having recourse to mimesis and inculcating it by social drill. But the road leading to sociality by mimesis is a short cut; and the fact that it may have been difficult to avoid taking it cannot blind us to the further fact that mimesis has been one of society's dangerous weaknesses. Mimesis is dangerous for the reason for which it is convenient. It partially anaesthetizes our human faculties of thinking and choosing, and this can dislocate a human society by paralysing human nature. If mimesis can work this havoc, "conditioning" must be a baneful *à fortiori*. For the difference between "conditioning" and social drill is one of those differences of degree that amount to differences in kind.

Most of the social drill that has made the wheels of society go round has, at most times and places, been largely spontaneous and unorganized. Even where it has been applied consciously and deliberately, as, for instance, in commercial advertising, in religious indoctrination and ritual, and in the literal military drilling of the Spartan or the Prussian parade-ground, it has not had the power to produce an irreversible change in human nature. The cake of custom, formed by social drill, can be broken, and, when it is, human nature emerges intact. To break it in defiance of strong public feeling in its favour requires, no doubt, the courage and resoluteness of a hero; but the saints and the martyrs have successfully risen to the occasion; and ordinary human beings have found it easy to break the cake when they have escaped from the social environment in which it has been formed. The Spartan abroad was notoriously prone to react against his Lycurgean training by going to extremes of licentiousness; and thousands of Germans who have emigrated to the United States after having been put through the mill of the Prussian Army have become admirable citizens of a democratic community. By contrast, the objective of "conditioning" is to deprive human beings permanently of their capacity to think and to will, and, since this is the capacity that makes us human, for good or for evil, "conditioning" is an attempt to destroy human nature itself. Perhaps we do not yet know enough about its results, up to date, to be able to tell whether or not its aim is actually attainable. We do know, however, that this has been the aim of its practitioners in our time; and we also know that the new science of psychology has equipped them with devilish devices which, in the past, were not at the drill-sergeant's, priest's, or advertiser's disposal.

Therefore we should stop to think, not just twice but many times, before we decide to commit ourselves to this psychological technique. This may look like a heaven-sent engine for hoisting us on to the ledge above us before the new military technique of genocide has had time to annihilate us. Yet the ledge on which the technique of "conditioning" would deposit us would turn out not to be the one above our last ledge. That last ledge was the ledge that we reached in the act of becoming human. We should now find ourselves on the ledge below that: the ledge reached by our ancestors when they became pre-human animals: the ledge, in fact, on which the social insects are still marooned. Instead of having taken a quick step up, we should have taken two quick steps down. The psychological machine that we had mistaken for an elevator would have proved to be a dejector.

A student of the social insects has thrown out an interesting suggestion.[4] The stupendous altruistic social acts that are performed willy-nilly by the social insects as we know them may have been originally performed, by these "conditioned" creatures' remote ancestors, as acts of free choice, guided by rational thought. In Hingston's mind this idea was perhaps no more than a *jeu d'esprit*; but a myth about a non-human order of living beings may throw light on mankind's past, as well as on our possible future. If it is true that our ancestors had become social animals before they became human beings endowed with consciousness and will, these pre-human social animals must have been "conditioned" to perform their social functions, as the non-human social animals—bees, ants, and termites—still are. The act that turned our ancestors into human beings must have been a victorious revolt against their hereditary spiritual bondage. It must, in fact, have been a successful assertion of a previously undreamed-of freedom to think and to choose; and these are the faculties that we now

[4] R. W. G. Hingston: *Problems of Instinct and Intelligence* (London 1928, Arnold), p. 268.

recognize as being the distinctive characteristics of human nature.

And what about the mythical history of the angels? Christian mythology represents the angels as doing God's will willy-nilly, like the social insects. But it also tells the story of a war in Heaven, when Satan rebelled against God and Satan's fellow angels took sides either with God or with the rebel. This story presupposes that, at the time of Satan's rebellion, angels possessed the freedom of choice that is possessed by human beings. Are these two pieces of angelology to be reconciled by supposing that the loyal angels were rewarded by being made immune, thenceforth, against the possibility of committing Satan's sin? If their nature was indeed changed in this way, was that truly a reward? Would it not be nearer the truth to call it a preventive penalization? Regarded from a human standpoint, it would look like a spiritual mutilation that deprived the loyal angels of their greatest previous spiritual treasure. And, if the fallen angels preserved their anthropoid spiritual freedom, did not this more than compensate them for having been cast down from Heaven into the Abyss? Are not these free fallen angels in Hell on a spiritually higher ledge than their fellows who have remained in Heaven at the price of being "conditioned"? Anyway, free angels, even though fallen, are nearer akin, spiritually, to us human beings than 'conditioned' angels are. Self-respecting human beings will assuredly endorse Zaehner's dictum,[5] that "Man is not an angel, and, in seeking to be one, he deprives himself of something that is essential to his being".

The freedom of the human self is a curse inasmuch as it is the source of spiritual evil in Man, but at the same time it is an inestimable treasure inasmuch as it is also the only source, in Man, of spiritual good. We recognize its value for us when we find ourselves under threat of being deprived of it. To be "conditioned" is a fatal evil in itself, even if our "unconditioned" fellow human being who is "conditioning" us is doing this in all good faith, not in order to serve his own self-centred ends, but in order to make our wills compulsorily conform to God's will as our human "con-

[5] R. C. Zaehner: *At Sundry Times* (London 1958, Faber), p. 168.

ditioner" see it.[6] God's will cannot be done by human beings at some other human being's dictation. Each of us has to try to discover for himself, through his own travail and at his own peril, what God's will for him is. And, since Man is a social being, each individual's peril and travail is also peril and travail for his fellow men. This is the inalienable privilege and penalty of being human.[7] We can escape it only by giving up being human, and human nature revolts against attempts to constrain it to make this renunciation. In the past, would-be tyrants have often been baffled by encountering something intractable in their intended victims. Fortunately for mankind, human nature is more mulish than it is sheep-like. This has been a saving human quality; but, until our day, our mulish human nature has never had to face the new psychological weapon that a present-day tyrant wields. In this new situation we may have to fight with all our strength to defend and preserve the freedom of our personalities which is our human birthright. We hold this precious gift not as owners but as trustees. Our free selves are ours to be used by us, not for self-centred purposes of our own, but in God's service. The angels' and the social insects' involuntary way is not the way for human beings.

If this is our decision, it commits us to the other alternative. Human beings will have to try to follow the way of the saints; and this is hard indeed. A human being who enters on it is involv-

[6] Actually, a 'conditioner' who is sincerely trying to 'condition' his fellow human beings to do God's will must have a self-contradictory notion of what God's will is. The 'conditioner' himself will be 'unconditioned' *ex hypothesi*. If he himself were not still in possession of his native human consciousness and will, he would be unable either to set himself his objective of 'conditioning' his fellow human beings or to work towards it. But he cannot reasonably suppose that God wills him and his fellow human creatures to be different from each other in kind. What is good for one must be good for the rest where what is in question is the fundamental structure of human nature. Therefore, on the 'conditioner's' own premisses, God must will the 'conditioner' to be 'conditioned' like his intended victims, and must therefore will him to be incapable of carrying out his self-conferred mission; or, alternatively, God must will the 'conditioner's' intended victims, as well as the 'conditioner' himself, to be 'unconditioned', and must therefore disapprove of the 'conditioner's' aim.

[7] See E. Gürster in *Die Neue Rundschau*, 13. Heft (Winter, 1949), pp. 140 and 141.

ing himself in a perpetual struggle and exposing himself to perpetual danger; and, even at the price of this tribulation, the seeker's goal will never be reached to the seeker's satisfaction. It cannot be, because a human being who rises to sainthood does not undergo a spiritual mutation. He does not become a creature of another species.[8] The distinctive characteristics of human nature are the freedom of the human consciousness and the human will, and this freedom is a saint's, as well as an ordinary human being's, spiritual instrument. The goal of a saint's endeavour is, not to sterilize his spiritual freedom, but to put it to work in God's service. This service is perfect freedom if it is perfectly performed; but the saint will be painfully aware of the gulf—invisible to ordinary human eyes—between his achievement and his ideal of perfection. As Berkovitz has well said,[9] there is perfection neither in this world nor in any other, but only in God; and this means that a human soul's—even a saint's soul's—fight with self-centredness will be unceasing.

If this is the truth, it tells us that the next ledge, if we succeed in reaching it, will not be a resting-place. Rest cannot be procured for human beings in this world by means of institutions, even if these are admirably designed for meeting the needs of time, and even if they are accepted whole-heartedly and operated in good faith.

"Whatever may be achieved, in the nearer or more distant future, in the way of institutions, organisations, federations, it will remain true that nothing achieved in history can be made permanently secure. There is no such thing as a human organisation that can be established 'securely' through being made weather-proof against the all-disintegrating action of time."[10]

---

[8] In iii. 232, I quoted, and endorsed, a passage in Bergson's *Les Deux Sources de la Morale et de la Religion* in which Bergson seems to suggest that to become a saint means to become something like a 'superman'. If this is Bergson's meaning here, I find, on second thoughts, that I do not agree with him over this, if, by 'superman', one means an ex-human creature that has become immune to the human failing of making a wrong choice. This immunity could be acquired only at the cost of forfeiting the capacity to make choices of any kind, wrong or right.

[9] E. Berkovitz: *Judaism: Fossil or Ferment?*, pp. 125–6.

[10] E. Gürster in *Die Neue Rundschau*, 13. Heft (Winter, 1949), pp. 141–2.

"The culture-cycle as a whole might be described as an alter-ation between rigid traditionalism and tendencies to disruption and chaos. And history knows of no resting-point in this up-and-down."[11]

Rest would also not be one of the rewards of a spiritual effort that succeeded in transfiguring human society into a communion of saints. Even in a saintly society the victory over self-centred-ness, collective and individual, would never be complete, and the effort would therefore have to be unremitting. This means that the next ledge will be the scene of a spiritual struggle that will not be less intense than the struggle to climb, from ledge to ledge, up the face of the cliff. Moreover, this conclusion about the condi-tions that await us on the next ledge above us raises a question about the ledge immediately below us. Perhaps this, too, was not, in truth, the resting-place that, so far, I have taken it to have been. Miss Oakley reminds us[12] that 'we must not ignore the gigantic effort of "Primitive" Man in rising from the sub-human to the human'. This effort is one that I had taken into account: it is the effort of climbing the precipice next below ours. But the success-ful performance of this feat may not, after all, have been followed by an age of torpor. Christopher Dawson points out that, even where a culture is apparently static, a continuous effort is required for the task of merely keeping the culture in that condition.[13] Dawson's observation would, no doubt, be confirmed from per-sonal experience if we could call as witnesses the elders responsible for the management of any one of the most primitive human so-cieties still extant; and, in the age of the Egyptiac or the Sinic uni-versal state, a Pharaonic or Confucian civil servant would assuredly have given the same testimony. Like the physicist, the anthropol-ogist recognizes that what looks, to an uninitiated eye, as if it were a motionless solid body is in reality a swirling legion of invisible dancers, each dancing with all its might for dear life.

The last word here may be left for a poet to speak. George Her-bert has perceived[14] that, when God at first made Man, rest was

[11] F. Borkenau in *Commentary*, March, 1956, p. 244.
[12] H. D. Oakeley in *Philosophy*, vol. xi, No. 42 (April, 1936), p. 190.
[13] Chr. Dawson: *The Dynamics of World History*, pp. 451–2.
[14] George Herbert: *The Pulley*.

not included among the gifts with which He endowed him. The
poet has also divined that this gift was withheld for a purpose.
God's intent towards Man, as Herbert sees it, was that,

> if goodness lead him not, yet weariness
> may toss him to My breast.

The intrinsic imperfection of human nature does, indeed, both
require and provide a spur. Yet struggle and danger—Man's two
inseparable companions on his journey through this world—are no
more than means to an end; and they are not the only means of
advancing towards the goal of human endeavours that Man has at
his disposal. The best means is identical with the end itself. This
end is goodness; and, though human goodness never attains perfection, not even in the soul of the greatest saint, Man travels best
when his imperfect goodness leads him.

If this is our conclusion, what, if any, practical bearing does it
have on the urgent question of our time? What are we to do to
save ourselves, here and now, in the alarming situation in which the
human race now finds itself? Try to become saints? And this with
the foreknowledge that, however far we may succeed in advancing
towards this ambitious spiritual goal, we shall never succeed in
reaching it, and, meanwhile, shall never win release from danger,
struggle, and weariness? If we agree that this spiritual endeavour is
the only alternative to self-annihilation *en masse* now that we
possess the atomic weapon, is not that merely an indirect way of
saying that mass-suicide is now mankind's inevitable fate? Is the
suggested alternative really a practical proposition? What percent-
age of the thousands of millions of human beings who have lived
and died so far has ever dreamed of aiming at sainthood? Can one
imagine *l'homme moyen sensuel* [the average sensual man] devoting
himself to an aim that calls for this degree of sacrifice, and that,
even at that cost, is impossible to achieve more than approximately
and imperfectly? Even if you could convince him that this is now
his only alternative to self-destruction, and even if he were to do
his best, is it conceivable that he would be capable of doing even
the minimum necessary for saving the situation?

One answer to these questions is that the very thing that makes
the pursuit of saintliness look like a thankless task is something that

also makes it a practicable one. The task seems thankless because it cannot be achieved perfectly, and the reason why it cannot is because the aspirant to sainthood does not cease to be a human being. Unlike the imaginary superman, the saint is not an ex-human being who has turned into another kind of creature through some mysterious mutation that is none of his own doing. He is a human being who has raised himself above the average level of human goodness; and, if he believes, and is right in believing, that he could not have risen without the help of God's grace, this is a further indication that the saint himself is no more than a human creature. Sainthood, thus described, is a well-attested historical phenomenon, and the human beings who have risen to this higher spiritual altitude have done so in different degrees. What some human beings have achieved in some degree must be a practicable objective for others; if grace has been offered to some souls, it will have been offered to all, whatever Augustine and Calvin may say; and any measure of success in approaching sainthood will have spiritual value. It is not a case of being asked to attempt the impossible or of being faced with a choice between all or nothing. The road towards sainthood is, in fact, an open one on which even the worst and weakest human being can set foot, though this open road stretches away towards an ever-receding spiritual horizon.

One of the first steps on the road is to acquire some sense of responsibility and to act on this by restraining one's own self-centred impulses. All sane adult human beings are responsible-minded to some minimum degree. Indeed, this is one of the definitions of what sanity means. One field in which ordinary human beings in the mass have managed to behave more or less responsibly is the handling of tools. In making his tools progressively more effective, Man has also made the misuse of them progressively more dangerous. In harnessing atomic energy he has now acquired a tool which is so potent that, if used as a weapon, might destroy, not merely a hostile army or people or merely the users themselves, but the whole human race. This new power has challenged the holders of it not to misuse it; and, since the dropping of the bombs on Japan in 1945, there have been indications that the holders of atomic power have been conscious of the new and awful responsibility that their possession of this power entails. The invention of the atomic weapon has made future resort to war a crime against the human race. And it is noteworthy that, since the end of the Second World War, the World's most powerful nations and governments have shown an uncustomary self-restraint on some critical occasions. They have given priority to their sense of responsibility for avoiding a world-war that would be fought, this time, with atomic weapons, and they have subordinated, to this paramount concern, their national *amour propre* and ambitions and even their ideological convictions.

On the road towards sainthood, this budding sense of obligation not to exterminate the human race is, no doubt, only a feeble and far-off step. The attitude is negative and the motive is largely self-regarding, since it is obvious that atomic war-makers could not exterminate their fellow men without exterminating themselves together with the rest. At the same time this step marks a notable breach with the habit of going to war, which is coeval with civilization. It is encouraging evidence of human nature's power to respond to the challenge of a revolutionary change of circumstances. It is also of great immediate practical importance, because it keeps mankind's foot in the door that opens into the future, and so promises to give time for Man's sense of responsibility towards mankind as a whole to take a more positive form.

If the first step on Man's road towards sainthood is the renunciation of Man's traditional role of being his brother's murderer, the second step would be an acceptance of Man's new role of being his brother's keeper; and, happily, this sense of responsibility for the positive welfare of Man's fellow human beings has already declared itself. It is, indeed, one of the fruits of the seventeenth-century Western spiritual revolution. We have noticed, in another context, that, in the post-seventeenth-century Western World, the progressive recession of belief in Christianity's traditional doctrines has been accompanied by a progressive advance in the practice of Christianity's moral precepts; and that, although this advance has been opposed, in the West itself, by the reactionary ideologies that have raised their heads there in our generation, the ideals of Howard and Wilberforce have, so far, not been driven off the field by the counter-ideals of Mussolini and Hitler, but have, on the contrary, been disseminated, in company with other elements of the modern Western Civilization, among the non-Western majority of the human race. As landmarks in the advance of this modern humanitarianism, we may single out the abolition of the slave-trade and of slavery itself, the abolition of barbarous forms of punishment, the humanization of the treatment of prisoners and lunatics, the establishment of old-age pensions and national health services, and, in general, the narrowing of the gulf between a poor majority's and a rich minority's conditions of life. This advance towards greater social justice through an increase in human kindness has been taking place in two fields simultaneously: as between different classes in a single country and also as between different countries in a world that is now in process of being unified morally and socially as well as technologically and militarily. The relatively rich minority of the human race has now recognized that it has an obligation to make material sacrifices in order to assist the relatively poor majority to raise its standard of living on both the material and the spiritual plane. Peoples that are still exercising political control over other peoples have now come, thanks to an American lead, to expect to pay for this political privilege instead of any longer expecting to draw the traditional profits of empire.

These practical steps towards the vindication of fundamental and universal human rights leave us still far away from the achievement of a communion of saints. Yet this conscious and deliberate advance towards brotherhood in a community embracing the whole human race is surely even farther removed from the involuntary sociality of the beehive and the ant-heap.

CONCLUSION

The problem of progress is infinite because it is also the problem of man. Have the thirty thousand years of the existence of Homo sapiens on the third planet of the star Sol resulted in the net improvement of this species and, if so, by what criteria of improvement, and what are its prospects for future progress? What leads some thinkers to maintain that progress is inevitable, and others to maintain that it is merely probable, or possible, or improbable, or impossible? By what formula can we compute the relative contribution made to progress in general by progress in science, in technology, in industry, in the arts, in government, in equality, in liberty, in goodness, in happiness, in spirituality? Is the whole human race involved or just some selected few nations? Are we progressing toward some fixed goal, or is progress by definition without goals? Is progress continuous or sporadic, spiraliform or by stages? Does it involve the amelioration of man himself, or only of his civilization? Is it the work of man, of nature, or of God?

The reader may already have succeeded in answering some of these questions for himself. He will at any rate have some idea of how Western prophets and scholars have dealt with them since the Renaissance. But no anthology can hope to cover all the ground involved, and none can hope to give a rounded presentation of all the issues, free of distortion and bias.

At least we may agree that we have not been exploring one of the minor themes in the history of Western civilization. Even if Carl Becker is right and the idea of progress is itself destined to disappear, a "temporary insight useful for the brief moment" in which it flourished, a mere few hundred years out of all the millennia of man's time on earth, the progressive faith explains much of the dynamism of modern Western civilization, As found in the Enlightenment, the thought of the French Revolution, German idealism, Anglo-French liberalism, Italian nationalism, American democracy, Utopian and Marxist socialism, Darwinism, and contemporary prophecies of world peace and world order, the idea of progress has inspirited most of the great political and intellectual movements of the last two hundred years. It is perhaps the most characteristic and pervasive theme in modern Western thought. For the scholar, at least, no matter what its future may be, the belief in progress has already won a secure place in the history of ideas.

A NOTE ON FURTHER READING

The best general history of the idea of progress in English remains J.B. Bury's *The Idea of Progress: An Inquiry into Its Origin and Growth*, first published in 1920. The American edition (New York, Macmillan, 1932) contains a valuable introduction by the late Charles A. Beard. An exhaustive philosophical analysis of the concept is available in Charles Van Doren, *The Idea of Progress* (New York, Praeger, 1967).

For the belief in progress in the early modern period, see Ernest Lee Tuveson, *Millennium and Utopia: A Study in the Background of the Idea of Progress* (Berkeley and Los Angeles, University of California Press, 1949); Carl L. Becker, *The Heavenly City of the Eighteenth-Century Philosophers* (New Haven, Yale University Press, 1932); and Charles Frankel, *The Faith of Reason: The Idea of Progress in the French Enlightenment* (New York, King's Crown Press, Columbia University, 1948). R.V. Sampson in *Progress in the Age of Reason* (Cambridge, Harvard University Press, 1956) discusses the vicissitudes of the belief in progress from Bacon to Marx. Of special value is Frank E. Manuel's *The Prophets of Paris* (Cambridge, Harvard University Press, 1962), which contains intellectual biographies of Turgot, Condorcet, St.-Simon, Fourier, and Comte, emphasizing their ideas of progress. Arthur A. Ekirch, Jr., has written an important monograph on the early development of the progressive faith in the United States, *The Idea of Progress in America, 1815-1860* (New York, Columbia University Press, 1944). For Marx's conception of progress, see especially M.M. Bober, *Karl Marx's Interpretation of History* (Second Edition, Cambridge, Harvard University Press, 1948).

Some of the best scholarly, as well as polemical, work on the history of the idea of progress over the last forty years has been done by theologians and Christian apologists. In addition to Niebuhr's *Faith and History*, see Christopher Dawson, *Progress and Religion* (New York, Sheed and Ward, 1929); John Baillie, *The Belief in Progress* (New York, Scribner's, 1951); and Emil Brunner, *Eternal Hope* (Philadelphia, Westminster Press, 1954). A good reappraisal of progress from the point of view of contemporary scientific humanism is available in Morris Ginsberg, *The Idea of Progress* (Boston, Beacon Press, 1953).

In addition to the works excerpted in this anthology, the reader may also wish to consult the conceptions of progress of such thinkers as Bacon, Perrault, St.-Pierre, Turgot, Priestley, Herder, Hegel, St.-Simon, Fourier, Mill, Mazzini, Darwin, Spencer, Bergson, Wells, Shaw, Spengler, Dewey, Mumford, J. Huxley, and Teilhard de Chardin. For another anthology of source readings on the idea of progress, see Frederick J. Teggart and George H. Hildebrand, editors, *The Idea of Progress* (Revised Edition, Berkeley and Los Angeles, University of California Press, 1949).